D0541604

HOW TO USE YOUR BRAIN

In the same series

Right Way to Play Chess
Track Down Your Ancestors
How Good is Your English

All uniform with this book

HOW TO
USE
YOUR
BRAIN

by
John R. Bews

PAPERFRONTS
ELLIOT RIGHT WAY BOOKS
KINGSWOOD, SURREY, U.K.

Typeset in 10pt Times by EMS Photosetters, Rochford, Essex. Made and printed in Great Britain by Richard Clay Ltd., Bungay, Suffolk.

Dedication:

I have grown to realise that the ideals and values which I thought were of my own origin, are in fact my inheritance, and accordingly I dedicate this book to my Mother and my Father.

Acknowledgements:

My thanks to Brian Gresty, Norman Murthwaite and Alan Roberts, for their support and encouragment, and to my family, friends and colleagues for their contributions and debate, without all of which I would not have completed this book.

CONTENTS

PART I

INTRODUCTION

Just think what you could do if you could just use your brain!

Why do we think the way we do and how can we improve?
Why do we each think differently, and does it matter?
Why do we make mistakes and jump to incorrect conclusions?
How does "sleeping on it" help solve problems?
How can you improve your own memory?
How can you programme yourself to be more successful?
What makes us disagree, and how can we reach agreement?
One thing which all human beings have in common is an ability to think. Day to day living, be it personal, social, business, or political, requires each of us to exercise our minds to one degree or another. We cannot avoid it, and the skill of our application not only determines our survival, but also our rate and extent of development. How important, therefore, to ensure that our brains work efficiently and effectively.

Does yours? Are you maximising your potential?

The only way to be sure is to check. But how?

You must examine your own thinking process, to weed out deficiencies and identify areas for improvement. You must do this yourself – it is YOUR brain. Nobody can do it for you. I can, however, show you how to do it, and I have done that for you in this book.

It is basically very simple. After all, you are already a thinker, so you will be familiar with many of the experiences I am about to describe. It is likely, however, that you have not previously paid much attention to the way you think, so although it may be simple, it will nevertheless be a useful opportunity for you to review your personal performance.

To help you, I have analysed the thinking process in a structured and logical form. I have identified pitfalls and causes of mental blockage, and defined a number of techniques to improve thinking performance. Each of these has been categorised and labelled for easier recognition and better control. This, in itself, can be very helpful.

For example, "Catch 22", is a boxed definition, being derived from the book of the same name. It refers to a fairly complex set of circumstances which would normally take some time, both to trace mentally, and to explain to others. As it is, use of the expression, which is now part of our general vocabulary, simplifies communication, and speeds up our thought processes. Many of the boxes that I have identified in this book may be used similarly.

Do not be tempted to skip any passages. The text may be simple, but the brain is very complex. The thinking process cannot be described in linear form without forward and backward referencing. It is only when you are familiar with the earlier definitions and rules, that you will be able to understand in full, the later detail. On completion, a full picture will have been presented, and the context of each section will then be seen as part of the whole.

This picture will include not only the processing of information, but also its receipt and transmission. Communication is vital. Human beings have the ability to transfer information to each other, which enables us to pass on ideas and develop new ones. Because of this, knowledge can be accumulated, so that new developments can be "added on" to the existing store. We did not have to re-invent the wheel to put a man on the moon. By exchanging information, each new generation consolidates existing knowledge, which is then used as the foundation for further expansion.

This is all very well, but the difficulty is that, to pass information to each other, we have to live with each other. And that is not easy. Even if we could communicate perfectly, we still have to overcome the complexities of human relationships. And we are all different. Although we exhibit many similarities, no two people think identically. Each is primarily concerned with his own well being. Although this is often achieved through mutually beneficial co-operation, conflicts of interest are inevitable. Handling these relationships is itself a skill which involves brain activity, and your self-examination will not be complete unless it includes this. That is why the later part of this book examines the way other people think. Understanding this is the key to ensuring that you can present yourself most favourably under any circumstances. Understanding emotions, both your own and other peoples', can also be very helpful, and a section on this is also included.

As you can see, the subject is complex; but not necessarily difficult. My approach has been to fragment it into simple stages. Among the questions that will be answered are:-

Why do we have emotions, and how do they affect our thinking?

How do you sell an idea, or commodity, to someone?

How do you know when to pay attention to detail, and when to adopt a broad view? How can this be used to advantage?

Why is positive thinking useful, and why might you want to switch it on, or off?

What is your "security zone", and "stress threshold"?

How do you cope with excess demands?

You will discover these answers, and others, as you progress through the book. It is intended to be a guided tour of *your* brain. The ideas, experiences and memories are all yours. My examples serve merely to trigger your thoughts. Try to use them in that way. I have deliberately made them simple in order to allow you the space to substitute examples from your own experience. That way, you will be able to match the contents to your own level and will thus obtain maximum benefit from this exercise.

Above all, remember that being able to think effectively is vital. It is the key to ultimate success in problem solving and the development of new ideas, and also holds the power to enable you to take control of your own destiny as emphasised in this well known poem.

> If you think you are beaten, you are.
> If you think you dare not, you don't.
> If you'd like to win, but think you can't,
> It's almost certain you won't.

How To Use Your Brain

If you think you'll lose, you've lost,
For out of the world we find
Success begins with a fellow's will –
It's all in the state of mind.
If you think you're outclassed, you are.
You've got to think high to rise.
You've got to be sure of yourself before
You can ever win a prize.
Life's battles don't always go
To the stronger or faster man.
But sooner or later the man who wins
Is the one who *thinks* he can.

Anon.

1
Why Didn't You Think?

Some years ago, during a very cold spell, a motorist arrived at a filling station and found that he could not remove the cap from his petrol tank. The lock had frozen solid. He decided to unfreeze it with the aid of his cigarette lighter. The result was disastrous. First his car, and then the entire petrol station, went up in flames. When asked to account for his actions, the man said, "I didn't think".

The mistake was elementary, and yet understandable. We have all made similar mental errors, though hopefully not with the same catastrophic results. It is no excuse, however, to say "I didn't think", for it is impossible not to think. Try for a moment to think of nothing – it's hard isn't it? A more accurate explanation would be to say, "I didn't think properly".

The motorist did think. He linked the heating properties of his lighter with the ice in the frozen lock. What he neglected to do was to consider the lighter in relation to the petrol fumes. He must have known what could happen. He had all the necessary information, and yet he failed to use it effectively.

Human error is a matter of everyday life, and occurs mainly because insufficient attention is given to the matter in hand. Perhaps then, all thinking errors can be eliminated by paying maximum attention to everything we do. Unfortunately, this is not possible. We are involved in so many activities which compete for thinking space that we have to ration the time available to any one subject. Even then, it is difficult to sustain concentration, and interruptions are almost inevitable.

Contrast this with computers. In general, they handle self-contained problems without interruption, and can be guaranteed to take into account every available piece of information. In addition, they are very quick and do not tire. The human brain cannot compete with this, and by comparison has many imperfections. This has its compensations however, for the imperfections not only guarantee our individuality, and give colour and depth to our lives, but also assist problem solving, creativity, and the development of new ideas. In fact, there are many ways in which it is advantageous that humans do not think like computers. If we recognise this difference, we can build on our strengths, and, if we also examine our comparative weaknesses, we should be able to reduce, or even eliminate them.

Thinking is a natural process which occurs spontaneously whether we choose it or not. The question is whether it is therefore outside our control, or whether we can consciously achieve improvements to individual performance. To answer this, let us consider the functions of the brain:-

   i) It is the focal point of the nervous system and interprets sensory impulses;

   ii) It co-ordinates and controls bodily activities;

   iii) It exercises the emotion, thought and memory processes.

So far as its sensory role is concerned, the brain acts on impulse and requires no conscious effort. Similarly, in its control of bodily activity, little conscious effort is required. There is scope for improvement, however. Take breathing, for example. It occurs naturally and is vital to our survival and development. We do not have to think about it. And yet, there is no standard level of performance. Most people breathe reasonably well, some badly, but few bother to develop and improve the way they breathe. Those who do, such as athletes and singers, experience great benefit, as do people who use controlled breathing as a means of relaxation in overcoming stress.

There are similar wide variations in thinking performance. We may experience changes in our own performance, and can observe in others widely differing levels of ability. This would suggest that there is scope for improvement and yet little attention is normally given to this subject. The aim of this book is, therefore, to review thinking performance. The analysis, and suggestions for improvement, should provide individual benefit, not only in connection with solo activities, but also in dealings with other people and in groups. In this latter context, the ideas will be of interest to managers, and others involved in business organisations.

My approach is to look first at the way information is stored in the brain and how this influences the way we think. The thinking process is, in the main, highly efficient, but is also vulnerable to error and mental blockage. The effects of this are examined by looking at the secrets of magic and sources of humour, as well as puzzles and the wonders of discovery.

In Part II, methods of overcoming mental blockage are considered, together with the opening up of opportunities for the creation and development of new ideas.

Part III examines the practical application of the thinking processes considered earlier, including positive thinking, negotiations and personnel management. In addition, the other two brain processes, emotion and memory, are also considered.

One of the purposes of thinking is to avoid thinking, or more precisely, the conscious effort of thinking. When, for example, a learner driver sits in a car for the first time, he or she is usually overwhelmed by the amount of information which has to be absorbed and acted upon quickly, accurately, and often simultaneously. An experienced driver, on the other hand, requires little or no conscious effort to perform the same task to a much higher standard, and often has space to listen to the car radio and talk to his passengers as well. The difference is that the experienced driver has had time to think about the requirements of driving and, having thought about them, and programmed his mind accordingly, he can forget about having to make any further conscious effort. He can drive without having to think about it.

In a similar way it is hoped that as you read this book and programme yourself with some of the thinking methods suggested, you will be able to use them without conscious effort. In this way you will avoid unnecessary mistakes and mental blockages, and will increase your thinking potential to assist problem solving, and the development of new ideas.

2
What Do You Think?

If somebody wants to know your opinion on a particular subject they will probably ask, "What do you think?". Producing your answer will involve three separate stages which may be looked at in terms of the way a candidate would answer an examination question:-

   i) You must first understand the question.
   ii) You must recall what you already know about this subject.
   iii) Finally, you have to produce an answer in a form which best matches the question.

The thinking process here requires not only recalling as much information as possible, but also discarding any facts which are not relevant to the question, and presenting the answer in a structured and logical form.

The best answer will be produced *only* if all three stages are performed adequately. A deficiency in any one will reduce the quality of the answer. This process is equally applicable to most thinking exercises, and in view of this, it will be useful to consider each of the three stages in more detail.

1.   UNDERSTANDING THE SUBJECT OF THE PROBLEM
You must start any thinking exercise by asking, either consciously or subconsciously, "What is the problem?", "What am I looking at?", "Have I got a clear picture of the subject to be considered?". This applies whether you are about to perform the simplest of tasks, or whether you are planning a major, complex project.

Even the most experienced individuals can run into

difficulties if they have insufficient or incorrect information about the subject to be considered. For example, doctors or motor engineers will have difficulty diagnosing problems if they do not have accurate details of symptoms. In the case of exams, if you misunderstand the question, you will obviously have little chance of producing a satisfactory answer, even if you are very knowledgeable in the subject.

You must have an adequate understanding and appreciation of what is to be considered and, in order to obtain this, it may be necessary to refer back for further information by asking questions, taking a closer look, or re-reading instructions.

2.   WHAT YOU ALREADY KNOW ABOUT THE SUBJECT

When you have established all the necessary information about the subject to be considered, you must ask yourself, "What do I know about this?", and "Have I seen anything like this before?". If you have, you will be able to draw on your accumulated knowledge and experience to produce your answer. If, on the other hand, your experience is lacking, the correct, or best, answer will be out of range, and this may lead to mistakes. For example, when I introduced my three year old son to a globe of the world, he threw it on the floor and kicked it. He hadn't seen one before and obviously thought it was a football. Similarly, there is the story of the office newcomer who managed to open the doors marked *push* and *pull*, but could not get his fingers under the door marked *lift*.

I have assumed for a moment that this thinking exercise is taking place within an examination room, because this replicates everyday thinking, in that your response is limited to the information contained in your brain at the time. There is no time – it is not permitted – it is not necessary, to seek additional information to assist your answer. That is the way your brain operates most of the time. In the case of more complex problems, however, some help may be necessary, and the thinking exercise would then be likened more with project work where assistance can be obtained from reference books, experts, etc. For the moment, however, let us stay in the examination room.

Clearly, the more knowledge and experience you have, the more information will be available to help you recognise and deal with new situations. This is why learning and experience are so important. They accumulate in our brains over a period of time to form a vast reservoir of information which is like a huge filing system, substantially indexed and cross referenced. It is amazing just how much information is stored there. We never have to produce an inventory of the entire store, therefore we have no need to consider its total volume.

To demonstrate some of the hidden depth of this store of information, let us consider for a moment about one particular subject, say "CATS". I have chosen this because it is likely that your knowledge and experience of them will extend back into earliest childhood.

What do you know about cats?

What do they look like?

How do they behave?

How many different types are there?

These questions will have brought a general picture of the subject to your mind, but we can dig deeper. Think of any experiences you have had concerning cats, and this will set your cross referencing system working. Your thoughts may now include associations with neighbours, trees, holidays, television, books, zoos, adverts, etc. The more you think, the more information you will recall. When you consider that this subject represents only a tiny fraction of the information stored in your brain, you can appreciate the vastness of the total store, not to mention its capacity for further expansion.

3.   PRODUCING THE ANSWER

Having obtained all the necessary information, the third stage is to process it into a usable form. In this context, the exercise may be likened to that of baking a cake. The ingredients are the two lots of information mentioned under the previous two headings, and the mixing and baking is the processing of that information. The ingredients are of little value without processing, and the processing is impossible without the ingredients.

The thinking process requires the effective matching of the two sources of information in order to interpret the new subject, and produce a response. To achieve this, the brain searches, sorts, calculates, rejects, tests and compares the available information. The brain is exceptionally good at matching this information even though, in objective terms, it may not always be correct. One example is that people induced to behave strangely under hypnosis often have, what is to them, a rational explanation of their behaviour. Another example involved my son who had a match when he decided that, because of its shape, size and colour, the world globe was a football. This interpretation was his best match based on the information available at that time. The answer was wrong, but the experience provided him with additional information against which to assess objects in future.

One of the keys to good thinking is being able to obtain the best, or at least, an acceptable match. There should also be some assessment of the likelihood of the interpretation being right, and the risks attached to being wrong. If the subject is familiar to you it is likely that you will progress quickly and with confidence. If, on the other hand, you are not fully acquainted with the topic, you should proceed with caution. The point is, however, that good thinkers should make proper use of the information available to them. For example, I remember a group of canoeists who threw a non-participating, fully clothed, member of their party into the river, before realising that he had their watches in his pocket for safe keeping. They knew that he had their watches, and they knew that submerging them in water could ruin them. What they failed to do was use that information effectively at the appropriate time.

We have seen that knowledge, and retrieval from memory, are important parts of the thinking process, but they are not substitutes for one another. Being very knowledgeable does not necessarily guarantee that one will be a good thinker. Young children, with comparatively limited knowledge and experience, often display qualities of good thinking, while some very knowledgeable people are, in fact, poor thinkers. Likewise with memory. Being able to recall information is not much use if it is not processed beneficially.

The way in which information is stored in the brain will be considered later, as will the techniques for improving memory. The main emphasis now is on the processing of information. Everybody can benefit from improved thinking methods, and the methods described in this book are equally applicable to people of all levels of ability, and in all walks and fields of life.

3
Think Straight

The teenager who goes on a cross-country walk in high heeled fashion shoes, or the motorist who drives recklessly through a built-up area, may both be accused of not thinking straight. This expression usually means that an individual's actions are out of line with some generally accepted rule or established practice. The offender may also be called silly for not conforming to these rules. Straight thinking, on the other hand, conforms to accepted standards and is, therefore, considered normal.

It is necessary for our further study of this subject, to have an appreciation of the differences between these two forms of thinking. In order to provide this, we must consider the way in which information is stored in our brains. This store of information is, in effect, the "accumulated knowledge and experience" referred to earlier. It is an essential part of the thinking process, providing the measure against which new information is tested and identified.

The storage process begins very early in childhood when we learn, from direct experience and tuition, a wide range of rules including:-

a) Environment: rain is wet; unsupported objects fall;
b) Communication: language; body signals;
c) Social contact: share belongings; play fairly;
d) Survival: look both ways before crossing the road;
e) Facts: Paris is the capital of France.

These rules are stored in the brain in the form of a framework, or structure, within which most of our thinking takes place. It is important to understand how this structure is formed, because it controls the way we think. In order to study the structure closely, it will be useful to have a mental picture of what it could look like. Imagine, first of all, that each single piece of information to be stored in the brain is contained in a little box. As the brain receives new information, the boxes are placed edge to edge in two columns as illustrated in this diagram:-

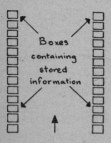

Each new piece of information is added to these columns to form the thinking structure.

Thinking Structure

This visual model may now be used to illustrate how the thinking process works. The new subject to be considered is passed through the structure and tested against the relevant bits of information contained in the boxes, until it is recognised and a solution is produced. This process may be illustrated diagramatically:-

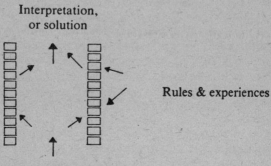

Thinking Process

Now let us consider more closely, the pieces of information which make up the structure. Although the input of information is personal to each individual, much of it is based on standard rules or common experiences. Most people will have many identical pieces of information built into their thinking structures. Because of this, it is often simple for one person to predict how another will, or should, respond to a particular problem. Similarly, it is easy to determine whether, in relation to the generally accepted rules, any particular action is right or wrong. When it is wrong, the offender may be challenged for not thinking straight.

Although many rules are standard and in common use, there is generally no standard programme of learning. Some subjects are of course taught in a programmed manner, e.g. reading, writing, and arithmetic, but in the main, learning experiences are not planned uniformly. Because of this, there can be differences between individuals, and imperfections do occur. The question of whether or not an individual's mistake is regarded as "not thinking straight", depends on whether he ought to have known better. If an adult had kicked my globe of the world, I would rightly have accused him of not thinking straight. As it was, my son could be forgiven for the identical action because of his age and obvious lack of experience. Indeed, I could have accused myself of not thinking straight for not anticipating his likely reaction.

We can, in fact, learn a great deal about our thinking process from our observations of young children. They have to absorb an enormous amount of new information in their early years. It is characteristic of children to be thirsty for knowledge, and they are constantly asking questions as they build their store of information. A great deal of information is taken for granted, but sometimes it is questioned and tested to decide whether it should be accepted. This is particularly likely if the new information conflicts with something which has been accepted previously. Sorting out the conflict is itself a learning experience.

Very obviously, a child's store of information is neither absolute nor totally accurate, but this does not deter him from attempting to project his thinking into new areas with mixed degrees of success. Mistakes are common, and often very amusing to adults. Indeed it is one of the favourite subjects for readers' letters to newspapers and magazines. They are also featured for entertainment purposes on television. I will mention a few such examples, to help illustrate the way our brains operate and develop:

a)   When a little girl was told by her mother that her family was going to move house, she said that would be difficult because it was stuck to the one next door.

b)   A little boy who was told that he was not allowed to bathe in the sea because he had a cold on his chest, replied that he didn't intend to let the water get any higher than his tummy.

c)   A little boy with a fascination for horses was encouraged by his parents to "Become a cowboy when you grow up" and replied indignantly, "You mean a Horseboy".

It is not difficult to identify the child's logic in each of these cases. The stories demonstrate how the boxes of information which make up our thinking structure may need to be changed from time to time to correct misconceptions. This process continues into adulthood but is less noticeable because it occurs much less frequently, and adults are less prepared to risk ridicule.

FRAGMENTED AND BLOCK PATTERN THINKING
Now let us look at some other characteristics of the thinking structure. The length of time taken to complete a thinking exercise differs from case to case. In some instances the response to a problem may be instantaneous. This may be the result of deliberately imprinting the information on the brain for rapid recovery, such as the mathematics tables learned in school. Alternatively, it may be due to casual familiarity with a situation such as driving a car. In both these cases, the thinking process is kept to a minimum. Or rather the *conscious* thinking is kept to a minimum.

Being able to respond quickly to familiar situations is of vital importance to the development of more complex thinking. The structure, within which the thinking process takes place, although built from the small boxes of information previously described, is able to use the information in larger blocks. The

brain is able to recognise the pattern of these blocks and thus
make more rapid progress than would otherwise be the case.
For example, consider again someone driving a car. Look at the
following table and compare fragmented thinking with the
block patterns:

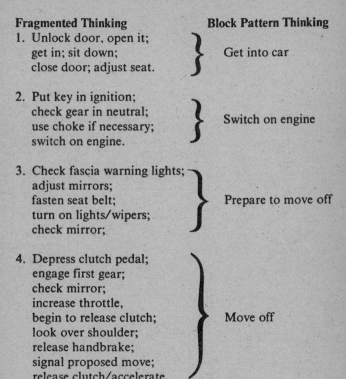

Fragmented Thinking   **Block Pattern Thinking**

1. Unlock door, open it;
   get in; sit down;   Get into car
   close door; adjust seat.

2. Put key in ignition;
   check gear in neutral;
   use choke if necessary;   Switch on engine
   switch on engine.

3. Check fascia warning lights;
   adjust mirrors;
   fasten seat belt;   Prepare to move off
   turn on lights/wipers;
   check mirror;

4. Depress clutch pedal;
   engage first gear;
   check mirror;
   increase throttle,
   begin to release clutch;   Move off
   look over shoulder;
   release handbrake;
   signal proposed move;
   release clutch/accelerate.

It can be seen from the right hand column that the whole
exercise can be carried out with minimum thought because it is
routine and follows easily recognisable block patterns. In fact,
the block patterns shown here can be further reduced under a
broader pattern called "Drive car". All the fragments are being
mentally checked, but only as part of the block pattern
framework. The process is illustrated here:-

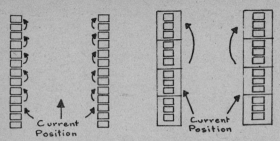

Fragmented Structure   Block Pattern Structure

If something out of the ordinary happens, such as the oil pressure light staying on, the driver's brain will switch from any unnecessary or less urgent activity, and will focus on the piece of the block pattern which did not perform to expectation. It does this in a way similar to television cameras when they switch from a wide angle shot to a close-up. Having focused on the new problem, in this case the oil light, the brain is able to use block thinking again in order to find a solution: check the oil level.

Our brains are constantly using block pattern thinking as a means of processing information quickly, and with minimum effort. Imagine, for example, if you had to resort to basic fragmented thinking each time you took a ride on the tube train. The system works extremely well, but is not without pitfalls which I will mention next.

BLOCK PATTERN PITFALLS

1.   Unexpected Occurrences.
Problems may arise due to the existence of a fault in the subject of the block pattern which you have not recognised because you are looking at the overall view. For example, you may sit down on a chair which collapses under your weight. Your block pattern will have told you it was all right to sit on the chair, when a closer examination of the chair would have shown otherwise. This can happen in any sphere of life at almost any time. Fortunately, however, it does not happen very often, and so we accept the risks in preference to being perpetually over-cautious.

2. *Jumping to Conclusions*

Sometimes you see part only of a pattern and complete the picture yourself. In the majority of cases this does not cause any problem, and it is something that we all do. We tend

only to recognise the phenomenon when it fails. You will have your own example of jumping to incorrect conclusions, and no doubt at some time you have mistaken the identity of a complete stranger, assuming them to be someone you knew.

Mistakes of this nature can run for some time. For example, I realised only recently, that an engaged tone on a telephone does not necessarily mean that the phone is actually in use, and that the phone owner is therefore at home. It could be that an earlier caller has made contact, and is unfruitfully waiting for the phone to be picked up. Later, callers will erroneously say, "I know you were in. Your phone was engaged".

Another form of jumping to conclusions arises where there is a strong link between two circumstances and they are perceived as one. You pull your handkerchief out of your pocket just as somebody else drops something on the floor. Or where there is some pressure to make a quick assessment – a passenger airliner flying through an active war zone may be mistaken for an enemy fighter. This may also be due to emotion which I will return to later.

Jumping to conclusions may have its problems but it is nevertheless an important extension of pattern thinking, and illustrates how the brain is constantly trying to speed up the thinking process to economise on effort.

Did you read the message in the triangle at the beginning of this passage? Did your block pattern recognition interpret the sentence as "Paris in the Spring"; or did you read it correctly as "Paris in the the Spring"? If you read it correctly and do not appreciate the point I am trying to make, try it on some friends and see how they perform.

3. *Crossed Lines*

When an activity in which you are not usually engaged coincidently takes you into normally familiar territory, you may develop crossed lines in your pattern thinking which can lead to confusion. For example, a motorist may find himself driving to work on his day off because he happens to drive along part of his normal route. Or you may answer the phone at home saying the same as you would at work.

4. Fade Out

The more familiar a situation is, the less mental effort is required to recognise the block pattern. This leaves room for other things to be going on in the brain. Just as a dimmer-switched light may be turned lower and lower to the point where it goes out, so a conscious awareness of a familiar situation may fade away. In short, you forget what you are doing. This can have disastrous consequences. Driving a car, for instance, requires concentration on the road, particularly in unfamiliar places. But what about driving in familiar areas. Certainly, if a new traffic signal is introduced, the people most likely to miss seeing it are those who are already familiar with the area.

Another problem of fade out is that routine actions of a familiar nature are not imprinted firmly on the mind, so that it is easy to forget whether or not the action has actually been carried out. Later on, you ask yourself, "Did I lock up?". It is unlikely that you would forget if more mental effort were required to perform the action in the first place. Problems of this nature tend to arise when other mental pressures are dominating our thinking. This may happen in conditions of stress, or when we have something particular on our minds. So called "absent-minded professors" are in fact concentrating their thinking on a much higher level, and relying on low level pattern recognition to handle familiar routine.

This fade out, or near fade out, is the explanation for boredom. The brain becomes totally uninspired by familiar routine and slumps into a state of comfortable stagnation. The condition does not remain comfortable, however, as the frustration of inactivity begins to surface. The remedy is to break out of routine and confront the brain with something new and challenging, so that it has to snap out of its semi-dormant condition.

CONCLUSION AND SUMMARY

Straight thinking is our most frequently used mental process. It has many advantages, enabling us to think quickly, and assisting us to move on to more complex matters without having to check on basics each time. There are disadvantages. however, which are to some extent inevitable, but in the main, can be regarded as within the limit of acceptable risk. If, on the other hand, you find these disadvantages are a source of frequent trouble, you may be regarded as accident prone, and you should consider some readjustment to your thinking structure. In short, if you are always "putting your foot in it". try in future to exercise a little more caution. Everybody else should continue to take these minor risks. The pay-off of high speed thinking is worth the occasional extra effort required to recover a mistake.

4
THINK FOR YOURSELF

Some years ago, the Queen Mother went into hospital for an operation to remove an internal obstruction, and the medical bulletin described her condition as "comfortable". The Queen Mother is said to have remarked, "There is all the difference between the patient's meaning of the word and the surgeon's". This is not surprising having regard to their differences of experience and position, and we shall be looking at the reasons for this. We will see that our personal experiences colour the way we view things, and that differences of opinion are common.

In order to look at the cause of these differences, it will be helpful to refer again to the framework, or structure, within which most of our thinking takes place. We have already seen that the framework is built from a collection of experiences and rules, and that many of these are standard and in common use. Early training encourages acceptance of these universal rules, firstly, because parental training has a strong emphasis on do's and don'ts, and secondly, because school training concentrates on the absorption of facts which are regularly tested and checked. Given this introduction to learning, it is easy for young people to imagine that we live in a "black and white" world, where there is a single, ideal solution to each problem. This, of course, is not true. Although many everyday problems are of the black and white kind, there is also a vast area of grey.

In many respects the black and white problems are easiest to deal with because correct solutions can be recognised, and will be universally accepted. You will know when you have the correct answer, and if you do not, you will be able to ask someone, or refer to a book.

Grey problems are a different matter because there is usually no clear definitive answer. For example, consider these two problems "Where should I go on holiday?", and "How do I design and build this new house?". The first problem is clearly a matter of personal preference, and success or failure will also be a matter for subjective assessment.

The second problem is somewhat different. The degree of success will more easily be measured by others, because they will see its development, and the final outcome. Some may even offer advice on the best method of approach, but it is YOUR problem, and YOU have to decide how it should be tackled, having regard to your own success criteria. In both cases there is a strong element of personal choice which can be taken into account *only* if the problem is fed through your own thinking process. The reason for this is that the mental blocks, which make up your thinking structure, include your personal experiences, feelings, beliefs, ideas and perceptions. These differ greatly between individuals, being more abstract in nature than the concrete facts and universal rules mentioned previously.

The next diagram illustrates how the thinking structure is made up of concrete and abstract mental blocks:-

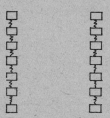

The square blocks represent the concrete facts and universal rules. The squiggles are the abstract, personal experiences, subjective ideas and perceptions.

The thinking structures of two separate individuals are shown in the next two diagrams:

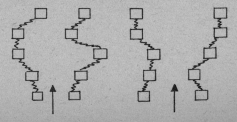

The square concrete blocks are common to both, but the squiggles are different, each being based on the individual's experiences and subjective ideas. These differences of experiences are likely to produce differences of opinion on particular grey issues. The overall differences in shape of these two structures, indicates the likelihood of the outcome of their thinking being different.

I will return later to examine the way *other* people think. For now, it is important to emphasise that our individual thinking is influenced greatly by the nature, range and extent of our personal experiences.

For example, the building of a new road or railway line often leads to conflicts of interest. There is, on the one hand, the public and commercial need for speedy and safe travel, and, on the other, a desire for peace and quiet on the part of the local residents affected by the scheme. Some may be directly affected and have to move away, while others will have to endure the inconveniences of living close to the new development. A further group may be concerned about the likely impact on the environment.

Clearly, if a random collection of people were asked whether, or not, the new road or rail should be permitted, their answers would differ, and would depend on their particular experience and position. Opinions would be coloured by the way in which individuals were likely to be affected. People not directly affected could afford to take a more objective view.

This is true of every sphere of human activity, and can be looked at in relation to the numerous groups to which we each belong. I will have more to say about groups, later, but for the moment I want to emphasise the way in which they can influence our thinking.

To start with, my definition of *group* in this context is "a number of individuals considered together because of certain similarities". Groups may be formal, but, in the main, will be informal and dispersed. In the previous example, there will be a group comprised of local residents, and another of potential travellers. Some people may belong to both groups, in which case they could have mixed feelings, or change opinion from time to time.

Let us consider some other groups, such as gender. We are

each of us either male or female, and this is likely to affect our opinion on certain issues. What is your view on sex equality, or ordination of women? Now take "age group". You may be a teenager, young adult, middle or old aged. What do you think about unemployment, early retirement, care for the elderly? You may live in a rural area. What do you think about development in the green belt? Or the price of houses for local people?

There are literally millions of groups into which you may be classed, and each of these has the potential to influence your thinking. The following is a list of some further groups, and you may like to spend a few moments considering the effect to which your membership of them shapes your opinion. Nationality, religion, employment – type and status, sport, social groups, family connections, hobbies, leisure and culture, charities, travel, health, etc. I am not suggesting that opinions will always "follow the party line". Indeed, this is clearly not true. There is, however, a strong tendency to look at the world through the eyes of the particular group member, and thinking is influenced accordingly.

Because there are so many groups, it is not possible for any two people to be members of identical sets. It follows from this that no two people will think identically on all subjects. You may share an opinion with somebody on one subject, but disagree entirely on another. I will come back to the problem of reconciling different viewpoints, but the main point to be made now is that other people will not always see things the way you do.

Indeed, there will be numerous occasions when other people will express opinions which differ from yours. You may both be able to quote examples in support of your own case, but there is rarely any guarantee that either side is absolutely right. Correctness is very subjective in these abstract areas. You may be right in your own terms, but the other person may have some good points which you should consider before confirming your view.

It is useful, from time to time, to review some of your own abstract thinking blocks because they may not be rational, and may be unduly influencing your thinking. Common examples of this arise from generalising untypical experiences. For example, an unpleasant experience with a policeman may lead you to dislike all policemen. Other areas which should be reviewed are those where you may have become subconsciously hooked on routine, and not bothered to consider alternatives, or where external circumstances may have changed, making a previously held view outdated or irrelevant.

To check your abstract thinking blocks, ask yourself, "What is influencing my attitude on this?", or "Why am I doing this?". I am not suggesting that you should make drastic changes, but some fine tuning is often beneficial. Don't forget, however, that it is *your* opinion that matters here.

Being able to think for yourself is both challenging and exciting. It adds colour to life by allowing people to have different viewpoints and opinions. Life would not be the same if we all thought identically, and politicians would soon be out of a job if we lived in a black and white world.

From an individual point of view, as each person's store of knowledge and experience is different, so too is the product of their individual thinking processes. Although we share many commonly held ideas, the individual differences make it possible for a person to think about ideas which nobody else has ever thought about before. New ideas and inventions originate somewhere, and mankind hasn't exhausted all of them yet! Any one of us with our unique stores of information can, therefore, produce the seed of a new idea. It is only a matter of spotting the right opportunity. I will deal later with some techniques for opening up new opportunities, but for the moment, the point to be emphasised is the importance, at the appropriate time, of thinking for yourself.

5
THINK OR THWIM

In 1869, a young Russian chemist, called Dmitri Ivanovich Mendeleev, tackled a problem which had been bothering chemists for a long time. The sixty-three elements which were known to exist seemed to have no special order. Mendeleev knew the individual properties of these elements, including their atomic weights, and wrote these details on separate cards. He placed the cards on a table in order of increasing atomic weight, and then noticed that the elements with a family likeness were consistently separated by seven steps. He had discovered that the sequence of atomic weights was not accidental, but systematic.

The solution to the problem was not complete, however, because as he progressed further up the scale, he came to an element that did not fit the pattern of family likeness. This was when he made his second discovery, for he realised that if he left a gap and moved to the next space, the pattern of matching families continued. He decided that the gap represented an element still unknown to man, and used his scale to predict its atomic weight and family characteristics. This prediction proved remarkably accurate when the element was discovered some time later.

What Mendeleev had done was to start with a foundation of known facts, and then project this thinking into an unknown area. This is an extension of structured thinking. We have seen how the brain uses accumulated knowledge and experience as a basis for testing and interpreting new ideas. The brain is able to recognise circumstances which are familiar, and can project thinking into unfamiliar areas by checking on the structure.

This structured thinking may be referred to as high-probability thinking because the thought process follows the most obvious line offered by the structure. Each stage follows a logical progression so that, at any time during a thinking exercise, it is highly likely that the next stage will follow a particular direction.

Ultimate success is never guaranteed, however. There will be occasions when the way forward is not clear and the problem remains unresolved. When this happens it is often because the structure, whilst not being able to provide an answer, is actually preventing a wider search for a solution. Metaphorically, it is sometimes said on these occasions that you are, "in deep water". So what can you do?

You can THINK OR THWIM.

What is *thwim*? It is not a spelling mistake, nor does it appear in the dictionary.

It is a keyword which opens up a different interpretation of the word THINK. On its own, the word THINK clearly refers to mental activity. Spoken together with the keyword, THWIM, there is a suggestion of a lisped pronunciation of the expression "sink or swim".

What has this to do with thinking and problem solving?

Simply this – you have to develop a different way of looking at things so as to be able to progress beyond the obvious, and through the structure.

In a recent T.V. adventure game, the teams had to construct and sail a raft, using metal drums, timber, rope and other materials left for them in plastic bags on the bank of the river. Despite several attempts, the teams were not able to obtain sufficient buoyancy. Eventually, however, it dawned on them that the solution lay in making use of the previously discarded plastic bags. When inflated, they provided the required additional buoyancy. Prior to this sudden insight, they had a mental picture of the plastic bags as packaging only. They needed to look at their problem differently in order to recognise the wider potential of the available materials. This exercise to sail the raft could, perhaps, more accurately be described as "THINK or SWIM".

You can improve your own chances of having similar flashes of inspiration, and I will explain how, shortly. In the meantime, it will be useful for you to have a picture of the mental process involved. If, despite exhaustive efforts within the existing mental structure, a satisfactory solution cannot be found, then it is likely that the answer lies outside it. When this happens, the structure acts as a mental block which restricts the area of search for a solution as illustrated in this diagram:-

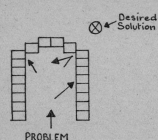

This is the position of the T.V. adventure team prior to their flash of inspiration.

If, for one reason or another, you suddenly become aware of the solution, you will experience a sensation as your thinking breaks through the structure to take in the new information. This is illustrated in this diagram:-

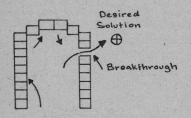

This is the position when the team discovered the alternative use for the plastic bags. The breakthrough was accompanied by a feeling of achievement and elation.

Once the breakthrough has occurred and the desired solution has been obtained, the mental structure re-forms to include the new idea. The "discovery" will now appear to be obvious and perfectly acceptable. Indeed, it may now be wondered why the solution was so difficult to spot in the first place.

Although I described Mendeleev's discovery and prediction as resulting from an extension of structured thinking, it is likely that it involved a breakthrough no less dramatic than that experienced by the T.V. adventure team. Retrospectively, his

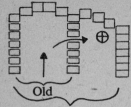

This diagram illustrates the formation of a new structure to take in the new information such as the team's use of the plastic bags, or Mendeleev's prediction of unknown elements.

New Structure

discovery seems logical, but he would have experienced a mental block if he had assumed that sixty-three elements was an absolute total, and that would have been understandable at the time.

This sensation, which is experienced at the moment one obtains a mental breakthrough, is the key to understanding the mental process involved. We have seen from the previous diagrams that there is a definite point at which the breakthrough occurs, and the connection of the new piece of information to the main structure produces a discharge which may be likened to an electric current connecting two terminals. The intensity of the discharge may vary from a comfortable tingle, to a severe jolt. In the case of the adventure team, the sensation was one of elation and self-satisfaction.

You may not realise it, but the experience of this sensation is already very familiar to you. It takes the form of laughter at humour, gasps of amazement at magic, shudders of horror, and thrills of achievement. The fact that these experiences are familiar to you, demonstrates that your mind is capable of breaking out of rigid structured thinking, which is in itself a key to creativity and problem solving. Being able to do this, however, is not the same as actually doing it. In the main, our natural experience of this "breakthrough sensation" arises as a spontaneous reaction to events. What is needed is more personal control to facilitate conscious choice, so that you will be able to recognise when a mental deadlock has occurred, and will know how to work towards overcoming it.

In order to examine the methods by which a mental breakthrough may be achieved, it will be useful to look, first, at the natural experiences with which we are already familiar. In the next few chapters, therefore, we will look at humour, magic, puzzles and discoveries. The common link between these topics is that they can all play tricks with the mind, and that is what we are looking for. Remember, "think or thwim", we need to find different ways of looking at things if we are going to break out of structured thinking.

6
I SUPPOSE YOU THINK THAT'S FUNNY?

Humorous situations may arise naturally or be contrived in joke form. In either event, the humour arises from a mismatch with the normal expectation which has been developed within the thinking structure. Ideas follow a logical progression. As we have seen, the structure is made up of blocks of information, some of which are commonly accepted ideas and practices, and some of which are based on experiences which are personal to each individual. Because of this, what one person sees to be funny, may not appeal at all to another. No wonder comedians have a difficult time entertaining their audiences. From your own point of view, your appreciation of any joke will depend on the degree to which you allow yourself to be drawn into the situation described. The more you relate to the situation, the greater will be the mismatch when it is revealed. The skill of a good comedian is to draw his audience into a situation, and then hit them with an unexpected revelation, or punchline.

In order to examine this process in more detail, it will be useful to analyse a typical joke. Take, for example, the old music hall classic:-

"My dog has no nose."
"Really! How does he smell?"
"Terrible."

This joke is based on the two interpretations of the question. "How does he smell?" The normal expectation was set up in the first line which suggested that, because the dog had no nose, it could not experience the sense of smell. The punchline is, therefore, a mismatch.

The mental process involved in the appreciation of humour can be illustrated diagramatically:-

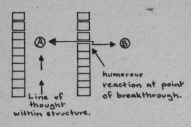

The line of thought develops within the structure to point A. Suddenly there is a revelation of point B which is outside the structure. A mental connection is made between these two points, which breaks through the structure and causes a humorous reaction.

Once the connection has been made and the joke is over, position B is understood in its own right, and there is a logical explanation of how it was reached. On its own, the logical explanation is probably not funny, as will be seen if we re-examine the previous joke:-

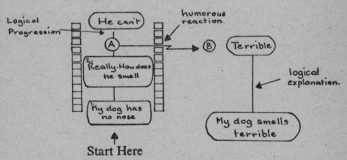

The comedian induces his audience with the first two lines of the joke. Having established a structure within their minds, he then forces them to break through it because the third line does not follow logically. The logical statement "My dog smells terrible", is not funny on its own.

An old joke may appear funny on re-hearing even though you know the ending, but will only be so if you allow your mental process to approach the punchline through the structure, as intended by the comedian. In this way, the enjoyment of a comedy act will be enhanced if you suspend your normal desire to think logically.

Apart from contrived jokes, humour can arise in the form of a practical joke. This is somewhat different from normal jokes, and is worth separate consideration, which will be helped with the aid of a practical example:-

A weight-watching colleague of mine, used to bring two hard-boiled eggs to the office each day for his lunch. One day, my other colleagues and I substituted one of the eggs with a fresh one, and waited for the fun. When lunchtime arrived, our victim began his ritual of cracking and eating his eggs while reading his newspaper. Chance had it that he selected the hard-boiled egg first, which he tapped on his desk until it cracked, then peeled and ate it without taking his eyes off his paper. Then he took the second egg. It did not crack as easily as the first, and he had to knock it quite hard before it finally broke. To his bewilderment, and our amusement, the runny contents spilled all over his desk and newspaper. What amused us most was that he didn't realise that he had been tricked, and tried to puzzle out how, after boiling both eggs for the same length of time, one should be hard-boiled, and the other completely raw.

This practical joke illustrates very well the subjective nature of structured thinking. The victim was unduly influenced by his previous experience. His actions were part of his daily routine. He had personally supervised the boiling of the eggs. In these circumstances, it was perfectly natural for him to react the way he did. A neutral observer, on the other hand, would probably have said that it was obvious that one of the eggs had been boiled and the other hadn't. Indeed my colleague was so locked into his thinking structure that he related his experience to every newcomer for the rest of the day, without recognising his mental error.

As you know, there are a number of T.V. programmes which feature practical jokes. The common factor is that what happens is not what the victim is led to expect. Or conversely, he is led to expect something which does not happen. One example which I remember involved a man in a white suit sitting on a park bench. He had green stripes painted across the back of his suit to give the impression that the bench had been freshly painted. He waited for an unsuspecting victim to sit next to him on the bench, and then he stood up to reveal the paint marks on his back. The victim's first reaction was to show some concern for the poor man with the ruined suit, but this quickly changed to concern for himself as he realised that he was sitting on the same offending bench. This incident greatly amused the studio audience.

Two interesting points arise from these stories. Firstly, the onlookers' enjoyment was not diminished even though they knew beforehand what was going to happen. Secondly, the victims behaved perfectly naturally, having regard to the circumstances as they saw them. Indeed, most of the audience would have behaved in precisely the same way.

These observations could disprove the theory I have already proposed, i.e. humour lies in the revelation of the unexpected. Certainly in these cases, the humorous event was expected, and the outcome matched that expectation. And yet they were still funny. There must be another explanation, although my earlier theory is still valid.

In the case of practical jokes the humour lies in observing the victim's reaction to the unexpected occurrence. This may take the form of bewilderment, embarrassment, amusement or even anger. One thing is clear, however, the more extreme the reaction, the funnier it will appear to the onlooker. If, on the other hand, the victim merely shrugs off the joke, it will stop being funny.

Looked at from the victim's point of view, his problem arises when he is let down by his structured thinking. This is based on his accumulated knowledge and experience, and relies on high probability as a means of interpreting new situations. When this fails, the subject will have to readjust his thinking to take into account the new information. He will also have to overcome the shock to his system in making the error in the first place. This is where the difficulty arises, because nobody likes to make a mistake; but it is even worse to be seen making a mistake. The victim is made to feel inferior. He made a mistake and the observers did not. This is the root of the observer's pleasure. He can feel comfortably superior as he watches the victim struggling to come to terms with his mistake.

This shows how much pride and value we attach to our individual thinking structures, and also our inherent competitiveness. We like to be right, and enjoy seeing other people make mistakes.

The remedy for the victims in these situations is, either, to shrug off the joke and readjust to normal as quickly as possible, or join in the amusement. Remember, the observer's pleasure lies, not so much in witnessing the mistake, as in watching the reaction to the mistake.

In addition to practical and contrived jokes, humorous incidents can arise quite naturally. It is said that to err is human, and I have already illustrated how making mistakes is an important part of the learning process. Humour is one way of dealing with some of these mistakes. I am not recommending frivolity, but there are occasions when a touch of humour will soften the trauma of a mistake, without reducing the effectiveness of the lesson.

I can recall an incident which I witnessed in a hospital casualty ward. It was very busy, with patients suffering from a wide range of injuries. In the middle of the chaos, I overheard two student nurses talking to each other as they changed shifts. It was clear that they were both new to the ward, but they were full of enthusiasm for the job. Some time later, I heard the ward sister ask one of the students if she had obtained a particular result yet. The nurse looked nonplussed.

"What result?", she asked.

"The urine sample I told you to take to the lab", explained the sister.

The young nurse put her hand over her mouth in recognition of her own error. "I thought you said LAV", she said "I've thrown it away."

The sister was stunned, but showed no other reaction.

"We will have to tell the doctor", she said, as they walked across the room towards the desk where he was sitting.

I did not hear their full conversation, but in a sudden lull in the background noise, I heard the doctor say, "Well can you remember what colour it was?"

This was not what one would normally expect the doctor to say in such circumstances, and yet it was very effective. The sister and student nurse both laughed at the hopelessness of the doctor's question, and the tension was taken out of the situation. They had both learned a lesson and were able to resume their duties immediately, without the diversion of an emotional upset.

Clearly, the use of humour in these situations is a matter of balance, but it is a very valuable human characteristic which everyone should cultivate to help cope with inevitable disasters. Indeed, this is the purpose of humour. We have already seen how mistakes can affect the thinking structure. If the mismatch is too severe, the structure itself will be rattled, and the individual will have difficulty recovering. If, on the other hand, the mismatch is dealt with humorously, the structure will only wobble, and recovery will be much swifter.

In summary, humour is a vital ingredient of the thinking process. Not only does it demonstrate the pleasures obtained from jokes and other controlled breaks through the structure, but it also helps to restabilise the structure when a mistake threatens to undermine it.

7

SO YOU THINK IT'S MAGIC

I once performed what I thought was a devastating card trick for my wife, but it left her totally unimpressed. You probably know the feeling. Don't worry though; we are in good company. Even the great Harry Houdini suffered an indifferent audience in his early days. He used to perform as many as twenty shows a day, each packed with magical acts, but few attracted any appreciation. Then, somebody told him that he was a poor showman, because he was trying to compress a thirty minute act into ten minutes. From that moment, he began to pay more attention to presentation, and often heightened the tension of his performance, by deliberately drawing out the conclusion of his act.

Presentation and patter are vital ingredients of a magic act because the performer has to create an atmosphere in which he is seen to achieve the impossible. For example, he may show you an empty hat, and then produce a rabbit from it; or a solid brick wall, and then pass through it. Whatever the trick, the magician relies on his audience's tendency towards high probability thinking to provide the foundation for their appreciation of his magic. His aim is to conjure up a picture in the minds of his audience, before surprising them by demonstrating that things are not what they appeared to be.

Only when he is ready, does the magician expose his final position, which confuses and delights the audience because it is so unexpected. There is a mismatch. This final position is impossible to get to logically along the path on which the audience has been led. The exercise is, therefore, magic. The more unexpected the final position in relation to the logical explanation, the greater will be the impact on the audience, and the more amazing the trick will appear to be.

This can be illustrated diagramatically, as follows:

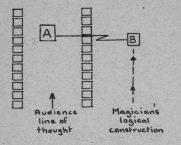

The magician induces his audience to develop a line of thought within a restricted thinking structure, up to point A. By this time, he has discreetly set up point B.

You will probably have noticed that this mental process is similar to that involved in the appreciation of humour. The performer has to instil a particular expectation into the minds of his audience before he can discharge it with a mismatch. There is a difference however, which is, that although the magician has a logical explanation of how he arrived at point B, the audience do not, and he should not reveal it to them, nor should they be able to guess it. Point B must remain unexplained if the exercise is to continue to be considered magic.

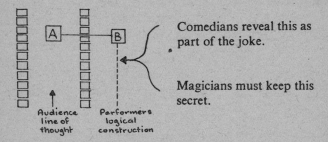

Comedians reveal this as part of the joke.

Magicians must keep this secret.

Consider again the practical joke with the raw egg. The perpetrators were fully aware of what had happened, and obtained their pleasure from their victim's confusion. Looked at from the victim's point of view however, there was an element of magic in the way the "hard-boiled" egg reverted to its raw state. This experience of magic arose because he could not explain what had happened. There was a logical answer, but his structured thinking prevented him from seeing it.

Most people enjoy magic. Some are content to be thrilled by the spectacle, while others press for an explanation, which should not be given. In any event, the explanation is often disappointing because it will be seen as a logical progression to point B, rather than a magical leap from point A.

There are many good books available on the subject of magic for those interested in performing their own acts. It will be useful, however, if I include in this text, the instructions for performing one particular trick, as this will enable us to look more closely at the mental processes involved. You may like to try this trick out on your friends. If you do, make sure you practise sufficiently first, so that your performance is polished. You will then experience first hand just how easily your audience can be misled. Or, looked at from their point of view, how easy it is to allow block pattern thinking to obscure reality.

THE DISAPPEARING COIN

For this trick you will need two identical pieces of coloured paper, approximately A4 in size, a drinking glass, and a handkerchief or cloth. Cut a circle from one of the pieces of paper to match the rim of the glass, and lightly glue it to the rim so that it seals like a lid. Now turn the glass upside down and place it on top of the second piece of paper. In this position, you will not be able to distinguish the lid from the paper on which it is standing. You are now ready for the performance.

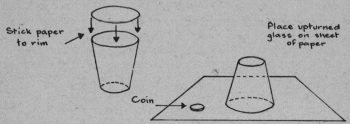

Stick paper to rim

Place upturned glass on sheet of paper

Coin

Show the glass in this position to the audience. Ask someone to place a coin next to it on the same sheet of coloured paper. Now cover the glass with the "magic" handkerchief and reposition the glass so that it covers the coin. Say a few magic words, and then remove the handkerchief. The coin has vanished. Replace the handkerchief, return the glass, making sure that the handkerchief continues to cover the coin, then remove the handkerchief and the coin has reappeared. Be careful not to let anyone pick up the glass or otherwise interfere with the equipment. You may wish to point out that it is the handkerchief which possesses the magic powers, in which case the audience may be allowed to examine that!

This trick relies on the audience making the false assumption about the drinking glass. It is a very familiar everyday object which does not require close examination. Block pattern recognition is sufficient. You could reinforce this mental block in their subconscience if you casually drank from an identical glass shortly before your performance. This glass would, of course, have to be removed from sight before the trick one was introduced. The doctored glass is, in fact, similar to an empty jam jar with its lid on. If you tried doing the same trick with that, not even the most gullible person would be deceived.

If somebody accidentally discovers the secret of your props, they will probably accuse you of cheating. But what is cheating? Most magic is based on cheating of one form or another. The only real cheating is that point B has been obtained in a way which is "not allowed" in normal structured thinking. Additionally, some tricks require the use of an accomplice, which may be regarded as unfair, but this is perfectly acceptable too, in appropriate circumstances.

There are other features of magic which I should also mention in relation to our consideration of the thinking process. Conjurers rarely say in advance what they are going to do, and they do not normally repeat a trick. This way the audience will not resist the apparently logical stages of thought induced by the conjurer. If they do not know where they are going, they cannot check whether it is the right way. They have little choice but to follow.

Often, the deception occurs early in the performance. The rest of the performance is the patter aimed at producing the illusion which is to be dashed. This is the lesson Houdini learned.

When the magic revelation is finally made, the audience will have no idea how they got to that point, other than by crashing magically through the structure from point A. They will be baffled and delighted by the revelation, but will still use structured thinking in their search for an explanation. In other words, they will go back to point A in their minds, and try to remember the precise sequence of events performed by the conjurer during the build up. This will be very difficult because their block pattern thinking will obscure any vital clues.

Magic certainly does play tricks with your mind. The point I want to emphasise is the sensation which is experienced at the moment of the mental breakthrough, out of the structured thinking. We have all heard audiences gasp at the startling revelations of magical performances.

8
IT MAKES YOU THINK

Throughout history, many people have enjoyed puzzles of one form or another. Perhaps the earliest example is that of the Sphinx, who asked travellers to Thebes a riddle, and killed them if they couldn't solve it. One day, the Sphinx confronted Oedipus with the same riddle:- "What walks on four legs in the morning, two legs in the afternoon and three legs in the evening?" Oedipus was able to answer immediately. "I know", he said, "It is MAN. As a baby he crawls on four legs, in his prime he walks on two, and in old age he uses a walking stick". The Sphinx immediately lost her power, and jumped from a high cliff to her death.

Fortunately, puzzling is not normally so hazardous, and puzzles are enjoyed for the mental exercise they provide and the feeling of self esteem which is obtained on their satisfactory solution. In the main, the puzzler's pleasure is derived from testing and extending the limits of his brain. For this reason, the amount of pleasure obtained usually depends on the degree of difficulty experienced. Very little pleasure is obtained from solving simple problems.

There are many different types of puzzle, including those which test accumulated knowledge, tests of logic, and others which attempt to mislead or tease. The thinking process involved in each of these types can be illustrated diagramatically as shown on the next page.

It is the brainteaser type of problem that I want to look at in this chapter. In most cases, the difficulty which these problems cause, arises because of the restricting effect of the thinking structure. Sometimes the puzzle compiler deliberately attempts

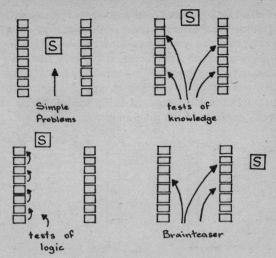

to develop a structure in the mind of the puzzler, and sometimes he relies on commonly held ideas. In either case, the aim is to create a mental picture which obscures the correct answer. For example, have a look at the problems which follow. The answers are given at the foot of the page.

1. You get ducks in cricket, birdies in golf, crabs in rowing, and bulls in darts. What do you get in bowls?

2. Name a footballer who played in the Third Division of the Football League and also captained England.

3. If you entered a darkened building with only one match and saw a gas cooker, a candle, an oil heater, and a wood burning stove, which would you light first?

---

1. Woodworm.
   In this puzzle, the compiler tried to build a mental picture by making a preliminary statement which, in fact, had nothing to do with the question.

2. Ian Botham.
   Botham played football for Scunthorpe United and captained England at cricket. The catch here was to make you think of football and thus block out any thoughts of cricket.

3. The match.
   The aim here was to concentrate your thinking on the burners, rather than the match.

Reflect for a moment on the amount of pleasure you obtained in finding the answers to these problems. If you found them to be easy, or if you read the answers without giving yourself time to think about the problems, it is likely that you were not particularly impressed. If, on the other hand, you struggled a little, you should have a greater appreciation of the answers, and may even have enjoyed being misled. These experiences may be explained with diagrams:

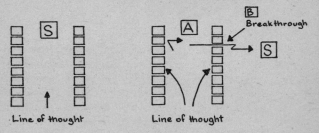

This diagram represents the position if you experienced no undue difficulty. Your thinking structure aided, rather than obstructed, the search for a solution.

In this diagram the structure resisted the search for the answer at B and yet the answer could not be found within the structure at A. The breakthrough came when it was realised that there was a fault, or misconception in the controlling structure. The recognition, or enlightenment, experienced on discovering the solution at B gives satisfaction and pleasure.

If you are now switched on to the type of catch intended in these puzzles, you may like to look at a few more. You will find the answers in the appendix on page 155.

1. A woman gives a beggar £10. The woman is the beggar's sister but the beggar is not the woman's brother. Why?

2. If you take 7 oranges from 12 oranges, what do you have?

3. How far can a dog run in to "Three mile wood".

4. If an American-owned plane carrying Japanese passengers crashed into the sea in Russian territory, where would they bury the survivors?

5. Divide 14 by half, and add 3. What is the answer?

6. If you walked 3 miles south, then 4 miles east, then 1 mile north, then 2 miles west, and finally 2 miles north, and found yourself back where you started, where would you be?

CROSSWORD PUZZLES

The satisfaction obtained on the successful completion of a problem is the basis of enjoyment experienced by crossword puzzlers in their daily rituals. The crossword compiler is an opponent, cunningly trying to fox the puzzler. The aim is not to defy detection totally, but to give the puzzler a good run for his money.

It is possible that you are already very familiar with cryptic crosswords, in which case the main points I would make are (a) the need to look at the clues from many different angles to avoid mental blockage, and (b) the pleasure that is obtained in eventually cracking a difficult one.

For those who are not familiar with these puzzles, the idea of cryptic crossword clues is that they contain two means of arriving at the answer; the main clue or definition, and a secondary clue which may be a play on words or other means of building up the letters to make the word. The tricks of the compiler may include anagrams, double meanings, words that sound alike, abbreviations and numbers. Examples of these are set out overleaf and are intended to demonstrate the need to find alternative ways of looking at things, as well as the pleasure to be obtained in discovering the solution. The answers and explanations follow each clue, so if you want to test your skill, cover the page and reveal one line at a time. Don't be discouraged if you find them difficult. Normally you would have the benefit of knowing some of the letters by virtue of completion of other clues.

1. Dream of frenzied canter [6 letters]
    TRANCE : A dream is a trance : frenzied means mixed up :
    frenzied canter means an anagram of canter.

2. That great charmer rattled a British prime minister [8.8.]
    MARGARET THATCHER : Prime minister : rattled means anagram of "that great charmer".

3. Floor covering in Redcar petshop. [6.]
    CARPET : Floor covering : in redCAR PETshop.

4. The old art school contains pointed arrows. [5.]
    DARTS : Pointed arrows : contained in olD ART School.

5. Saw a sailing ship. [6.]
    CUTTER : saw (used for cutting) : sailing ship.

6. Took on the enemy though already occupied. [7.]
    ENGAGED : Took on the enemy : already occupied.

7. Someone who throws a jug. [7.]
    PITCHER : someone who throws (pitches) : jug.

8. Sounds like the only uncertainty has all gone. [4.3.]
    SOLD OUT : all gone : sounds like "sole doubt".

9. Permission for half a dozen to go to South Africa. [4.]
    VISA : permit = visa : half a dozen = VI (roman numerals) + South Africa = S.A.

10. Embraces 150 snakes [6.]
    CLASPS : embraces : 150 = CL (roman numerals) + snakes = ASPS.

11. Hooded jacket king hid in a tree [6.]
    ANORAK : hooded jacket : a tree = AN OAK : king is rex or R hidden in an oak = an oRak.

12. Man loses right dress [4.]
    ROBE : Man's name Robert : right = rt : Robert loses rt = robe : a dress = robe.

The best way to develop your skill at crosswords is to attempt one each day and check the solution later. This way you learn how the compilers' minds work and you will become less likely to be caught out. For example the first time I saw reference to "flower", I concentrated on names of plants, whereas the compiler was referring to a river, which flows.

Further puzzles

Before leaving this chapter you may like to try another, more difficult, problem:-

A castaway is stranded on an island which is surrounded by shark-infested waters. The island is covered with inflammable trees and bushes, and a fire has broken out at the northern end of the island. The wind is blowing from the north, and unless it changes direction, is likely to spread across the entire island. What action should the castaway take to avoid this peril?

You will find the answer in the appendix on pages 155/6, together with a number of other problems for you to try.

Remember when tackling these, and other problems, to look for a variety of methods of approach.

9
I THINK I'VE GOT IT

Over two thousand years ago, Archimedes was given a problem by the Greek King Hiero. The King had ordered a new gold crown, but he suspected his jeweller of stealing part of the gold, and replacing it with cheaper silver. Archimedes knew that metals have different weights. A cube of gold is heavier than a similar cube of silver. He could weigh the crown but could not calculate its volume without melting it down, which would ruin it.

Everybody knows that Archimedes was taking a bath one day when he noticed that the water level rose as he immersed his body. He suddenly realised that he could use this discovery to measure the precise volume of the King's crown, and he leapt out of his bath shouting "Eureka. I've found it."

When a problem has been bothering somebody for a long time and they appear to have exhausted all avenues in the search for a solution, a chance happening can throw new light on the problem, and perhaps point to an answer. Such enlightenment is often greeted with great excitement and pleasure similar to that experienced by Archimedes, and indeed the T.V. adventure team mentioned on page 35. This experience can be illustrated diagramatically:-

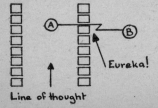

The thinking is concentrated within the structure at A. Something happens to bring B. into vision, and there is an immediate reaction as the breakthrough is achieved.

These discoveries will be dealt with in more detail in later chapters, but a number of observations should be made at this point:-

1) The discovery may result from a conscious effort to seek it out, e.g. the buoyancy of the plastic bags.

2) The discovery may be the result of a subconscious mulling over of a problem, and may arise during some totally unrelated activity, e.g. Archimedes in his bath.

3) The discovery may precede the recognition of a defined problem, e.g. Percy Shaw's invention of the catseye.

In each of the latter two cases, the discovery arose from a combination of unrelated activities. Archimedes did not take a bath in order to solve the problem of the King's crown, nor did Percy Shaw drive in the dark in order to invent a means of illuminating his route. It was chance that set up the common link, and genius that recognised it.

This combination of unrelated activities brings into consideration another dimension of structured thinking. Up to this point, we have looked at a single structure within which most of our thinking takes place. This structure is designed to deal with a particular issue, or subject. For example, in an earlier chapter we recalled as much as possible about CATS. When a different subject is considered, a different structure, or substructure, is formed. In other words, our brains can produce many different substructures, the chosen one depending on the subject to be considered.

There will almost inevitably be some overlap between individual substructures. For example, if we turn our attention to DOGS, then our brains can immediately develop a substructure to enable us to deal with problems such as "Are dogs dangerous?", "Are they useful?", "Are dogs man's best friend?". These matters are different from those considered under the heading, CATS. Nevertheless clearly there are areas common to both, e.g. family pets. This overlap can be illustrated diagramatically:-

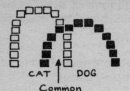

CAT   DOG

Common

It can be seen that these two subjects have their own individual characteristics as well as areas of common interest.

Now you may say that I have deliberately selected two subjects with an obvious common interest. But if you select at random any two separate subjects, it is likely that there is some way in which the two could be connected. For example, as I glance around me at this moment, I can see a piano and some goldfish.

What do they have in common? How can they be connected? First of all, I have noticed that the fish respond to the vibrations of the piano when it is played (perhaps it is something to do with scales!). Could a fishtank be built into the face of the piano to make it more attractive and interesting? Could I compose a piece of music with goldfish as the theme, or maybe the fishtank could have a musical box attached to it. Alternatively, why not have a model piano in the fishtank instead of the usual underwater models like wrecked ships? This could lead to having a whole range of household furniture models in the fishtank.

Clearly many of these ideas are more than a little eccentric, but they do demonstrate how links between different subjects can be developed. I will return to this process later, but will now consider two interesting phenomena which arise from the brain's ability to produce substructures to deal with each individual subject.

The first relates to the manner in which the brain stores information. For example, if you have ever had to manage without your wristwatch, you have probably had to ask the time on a number of occasions in order to regulate your activities. You may be good at gauging the passage of time, in which case you probably make a conscious effort to store, and monitor the information. Difficulties can arise, however, if having been told the time, you store the information away with the particular subject you were thinking about when you needed to know the time. For example, suppose you plan to go out at 6.30pm. You may ask, and be told that the time is 5.10pm. You think to yourself that you have got an hour and twenty minutes to get ready. In the meantime, you think you would like to see a particular programme on T.V. You know what time the programme starts, but what time is it now? You cannot remember the time that you have just been told because you have filed it away in your brain under the heading, "Going out at 6.30pm". The point that I want to make is that it is possible for you to have the required information in your brain, but for it to be locked up and not readily retrievable.

The second experience to be considered is the breakthrough which occurs when two separate ideas, or channels of thought, suddenly come together. For example, have you ever been exploring an unfamiliar town or rural area, when your venture brought you back to a place you already knew. Maybe you did not recognise it immediately because your approach was from an unfamiliar direction. The discovery probably gave you a feeling of pleasure, or even excitement.

Similar experiences can arise in identifying someone who is known to you. If you ever encounter a person whom you already know, but in a context which is different from that to which you are normally accustomed, it is likely that you will not recognise him immediately. You may get some signals which point to a connection, but will not necessarily recognise them until the evidence becomes overwhelming. The feelings experienced at the moment of realisation are similar to those considered earlier when breaking through structured thinking.

While on the subject of discovery and invention, and in order to illustrate again the coming together of two separate experiences, I will mention an idea which came to me some years ago. Our office car was kept in a walled yard which had a narrow access onto a main road. Getting out of the yard was a precarious manoeuvre, because the nose of the car had to be poked out into the road before full visibility could be obtained. Although I didn't drive at the time, the problem bothered me. Some time later I noticed a mirror sited opposite a similarly restricted access, and this started my mind thinking again. There was nothing new about this mirror. There are many of them all over the country. I thought about having one sited opposite our office, but decided this was impracticable. Then I thought of placing the mirror on the car itself. Cars have rear-view mirrors: Walls have mirrors to provide round-the-corner vision: Why shouldn't cars have mirrors to enable motorists to see round corners.

The idea was quite simple. All that was required was an adjustment to a front near-side wing mirror, which could be activated by the driver whenever required. During the next few days I was amazed at the number of occasions which arose when it would have been useful to have such an accessory on the car.

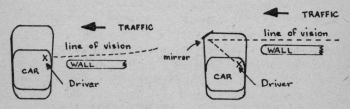

I did not develop this idea beyond the prototype stage, but have since seen a Land Rover fitted with one. The experience does demonstrate, however, that new ideas do not necessarily start from a deliberately defined point. Nor is there necessarily a specific problem to be solved; it may be no more than a matter of inconvenience. Successful improvement may come, not from sitting down working out a solution, but from waiting and watching subconsciously for coincidence to bring the necessary pieces together. The key to creative thinking is to be able to recognise when this happens.

Our brains are constantly cross-fertilizing ideas, and the results can often be rewarding and even profitable. Edward Bals was driving along the road one day when the wheels of a passing vehicle flung wet road dirt on to his windscreen. His first reaction was one of annoyance, but then he realised that the principle could be used to develop an agricultural spraying machine, which he did very successfully.

There is no end to this source of new ideas, and the later chapters of this book will help you to increase your own chances of similar success.

10
THINK BACK

Thinking back, or recapping, is often a useful exercise in a learning, or developing, situation. It refreshes the memory, and provides a broader picture within which the context of each individual stage can be better understood.

This is, perhaps, an appropriate moment to recap our consideration of the thinking process. We began by recognising that, although thinking is a natural ability, performances can be improved by examining the way we think and developing technique. We looked at the two essential elements which enable us to compare the matter currently under consideration, with our accumulated knowledge and experience. The third element, the thinking process itself, controls the comparison by matching the available information in order to produce an assessment or interpretation.

Next, we looked at straight thinking, which is predictable, highly probable and tightly structured. The main advantages of this type of thinking are speed and economy of effort, but there are also disadvantages such as mental blockage and jumping to incorrect conclusions.

The importance of being able to think for yourself was considered, when it was also recognised that people think differently because their experiences are individually unique. These differences become most apparent when the subject matter is abstract, or grey, rather than factual, concrete, or black and white. (I will, however, qualify this in a later chapter.)

We returned to the problems which arise from tightly structured thinking and particularly the need, on occasions, to break out of the structure. We dealt extensively with the effects of breaking through the structure and the variety of sensations which are experienced on such occasions. The principle of the sub-structure was then introduced, demonstrating the ability of the brain to file, and cross reference, information into an infinite number of different subjects.

Having reached this point, we now have a general picture of the complex nature of the function of the brain. It is recognised that straight thinking, within a developed structure, forms a vital part of our total thinking process and therefore must be included in any plan to improve thinking capability. Usually it produces perfectly satisfactory results, but it does have limitations which may block the discovery of a better or more elegant solution.

The next stage is to examine methods of breaking through the structure in order to develop new ideas, or overcome mental blocks in problem solving. We have already seen, from our consideration of humour and magic, that this can be done. What we need to do, now, is understand how to control it. Structured thinking is important, but it does unnecessarily constrain the area of search for solutions and new ideas. We have to find a way of opening up the structure, thus permitting new opportunities to become more freely available. This is the prime concern of the next part of the book.

PART II

INTRODUCTION

THINK ABOUT IT

You will recall that under the heading "Think or Thwim", we considered the mental process involved when the desired solution to a problem lies outside the thinking structure. This is illustrated diagramatically as follows:

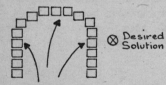

The structure is blocking any opportunity to discover the desired solution.

The aim, now, is to consider ways of opening up the structure to overcome this problem. This will be dealt with under five distinct chapter headings as follows:-

A. THINK AGAIN:-	Avoid narrow, or blinkered vision.
B. THINK BROADLY:-	Consciously widen vision of problem.
C. THINK IT THROUGH:-	Try to break through the structure.
D. INVERTED THINKING:-	Turn problem upside down or inside out.
E. KEEP THINKING:-	Avoid reaching premature conclusions.

Each of these methods will now be considered in greater detail.

11
THINK AGAIN

DEFINING A PROBLEM

Great care should be taken from the outset when defining a problem, or identifying an issue to be considered. The reason for this is that, as soon as you decide what the problem is, your brain produces an appropriate structure within which the problem will be tackled. If the problem has been incorrectly defined, the structure will limit the area of search, and may block the discovery of an ideal solution (see diagram).

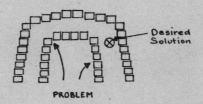

Let us consider a simple example of this. Imagine that you are driving your car to a meeting and that it breaks down en route. What is the problem? Is it the car, or is it the meeting? It is probably both, but maybe one is more pressing than the other. If it is the car, do you try to identify the cause of the breakdown, or do you try to summon help? The next diagram illustrates how, in selecting any one of these starting points, the structure restricts the thought process and blocks any wider search.

There are, of course, other starting points to this problem and each may lead the thought process in a particular direction to the exclusion of the others. If, on the other hand, the problem is

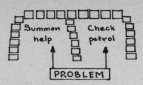

considered in its widest context, then any, or all of the following possibilities may be considered:-

a) Check the engine.
b) Check the petrol.
c) Call a taxi.
d) Walk to the nearest garage.
e) Call a motoring organisation.
f) Call the person you were intending to meet.
g) Flag down a passing car.
h) Try to restart the car.

Clearly, there are other possibilities which could also be considered. That is not to say that they are equally acceptable but they should not be discounted until one of the solutions is successfully acted upon.

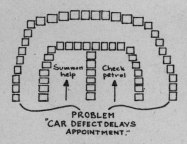

This diagram shows that the wider structure allows a wider area of search, so that many alternatives can be considered before the best solution is chosen and acted upon.

I chose this simple problem, so that the principles could be illustrated clearly. These principles apply equally to more complex problems where it may be less obvious that the chosen starting point has limited potential. In all cases, however, care must be taken when defining the problem to be tackled.

If, when tackling a problem, you are drawn into selecting an unjustifiably narrow starting point, it may be advisable to "think again". Be particularly cautious in the following circumstances which are classic traps for the unwary narrow thinker:-

    a)   Correcting a fault.
    b)   Adopting a favourite angle.
    c)   Arrogance.
    d)   Problems posed by others.
    e)   Recurring problems.
    f)   Coincidence.

Each of these circumstances will be considered in turn.

a) CORRECTING A FAULT. If the problem is that a fault, or error has occurred, then it is likely that attention will be focused on trying to correct that fault, rather than looking for the best way to achieve the desired objective. Successful correction of the fault may return the situation to its former state, but in doing so, an opportunity for improvement may be missed.

An example of this type occurred when local council workmen had to dig a hole in the busy main street. Local diversions were introduced and a temporary one-way system brought into being. There was an unplanned delay in making good the road surface, during which time it was observed that the traffic was flowing more freely than usual. Because of this, the one-way system was made permanent.

The Council engineers were obviously good thinkers – at least on this occasion. But why had this benefit not been spotted on the numerous occasions the road had been closed previously. The answer is probably that problem was viewed in terms of the effect of the hole in the road on two-way traffic, instead of the wider definition of "traffic flow".

b) FAVOURITE ANGLE. There may be occasions, when presented with a problem, where your attention is drawn in a particular direction because the area is familiar or pleasing to you. Your knowledge and enthusiasm for the chosen direction may lead you to a solution. On the other hand, it may not, and even if it does, you may have missed a better opportunity.

In the medical field, it could be that a surgeon would look for a surgical remedy, while a physician might suggest medical treatment.

The warning is that your favourite way of tackling a particular problem is not necessarily the best way, and your enthusiasm for it may detrimentally obscure a wider view.

c) ARROGANCE. It is easy for an "expert" to claim at the outset that he *knows* that the solution lies in a particular direction. It becomes progressively more difficult to defend this position if circumstances do not develop as expected. The expert then becomes so obsessed with self preservation, that he refuses to consider any ideas or suggestions which lie outside his narrow-minded vision. His mental efforts are then concentrated on trying to save face rather than trying to solve the problem. A negative attitude then develops as he attempts to destroy any suggestions made by "non-experts", and pays less attention to the search for a solution.

People who make instant, or premature, assessments of a problem fall into this category. In one of the adventures of Sherlock Holmes, the master detective says that people who try to act with insufficient facts or data will try to match those facts with an established theory, whereas if they wait until they have obtained more data, they will be able to develop a theory to match the facts.

d) PROBLEMS POSED BY OTHERS. When taking on a problem from another person, be careful that he does not unduly predetermine the structure within which you are to seek a solution. Clearly, there must be some guidance as to the nature of the problem and criteria for success, but you should not allow this to be over restrictive.

When King Soloman was asked to decide which, of two women, was the true mother of a baby, he was not drawn into making a straight decision as the people expected. Instead, he said that the baby should be cut in half so that the claimant mothers could have half each. This solved the problem, but not in the way envisaged by those who had set it. The imposter agreed to the King's suggestion, while the true mother declined, preferring the other woman to have her child rather than see it harmed.

e) RECURRING PROBLEMS. If some item of equipment is

rendered unworkable by a recurring problem, it is likely that you will focus attention on that particular spot when the equipment next breaks down. This is understandable and perfectly justified as it demonstrates the value of experience. But what happens if the trouble does not arise from the usual fault? You may be so convinced that it does, that you block out any thought of an alternative explanation.

f) COINCIDENCE. Confusion can arise when two separate actions appear to be "cause and result" when, in fact, they are totally unconnected. Such coincidences can fool you into restricting your field of vision for a solution. It may happen in an everyday situation. You pull a handkerchief out of your pocket just as somebody else drops some loose change on the ground. In this example, you can quickly identify the cause of the confusion and correct your thinking immediately. When dealing with more complex problems, however, the coincidence may carry a lot of weight in your perception.

CONCLUSION. Being aware of these potential traps should help you to avoid most of them. It is almost inevitable, however, that you will be caught at one time or another, and that this will result in mental blockage. When this happens, the remedy is to start at the beginning and think again. This time try to identify, and avoid, the particular trap in which you were caught. When starting again, keep the structure as broad as possible by following the suggestions made in the next chapter.

12
THINK BROADLY

We have just seen how important it is to avoid taking too narrow a view of a problem from the outset. The aim of this chapter is to consider how to broaden the opening view as much as possible. This is illustrated in this diagram:-

Make a conscious effort to widen the opening view.

The following methods may be used to achieve this:-

a) TIME ALLOCATION

It is often beneficial to allow a certain amount of time at the commencement, in order to think of as many different ways of tackling the problem as possible. A keyword should be used to record each proposed angle, but no consideration should be given to any, until the preparation time has elapsed and the list is complete. In the case of the breakdown of the car we considered earlier, you will recall that six or seven possible angles were listed. Each of these could be considered in some detail before the preferred course of action is settled upon. The amount of time available for action may, of course, be a limiting factor, but will not always be so.

b) PREFIX NUMBER OF ANGLES

This method is very similar to the previous one, the difference being that the controlling factor is the NUMBER of angles you decide to look for. This could be anything between, say, five and ten. Going back to the problem of the car breakdown, I am sure it would be possible to think of a few more angles than those listed.

You may feel critical of these two methods which seem somewhat arbitrary. It should be remembered that they are designed to increase the number of angles to be considered, and so the targets should be set to produce a reasonable optimum, care being taken not to cut off the flow of new ideas prematurely.

The benefit of these methods is largely self evident. In particular they will stop you running off on a wild goose chase in pursuit of a solution which looks very attractive on the surface but which turns out to have limited potential. Such an attractive opening will tend to blinker your view of the problem, and obscure more fruitful alternatives.

c)   FOR, AGAINST AND NEUTRAL

Another way to open up the start position is to list, not only the advantages and disadvantages, but also the neutral consequences of proposed actions. It is, perhaps, normal to consider the pros and cons of any issue, but the inclusion of neutrals widens the dimension, and they may even be developed into a deciding factor. The numerous points are listed under headings, FOR, AGAINST, and NEUTRAL, or F.A.N. The result is a broad viewpoint which can be viewed diagramatically as a fan:-

This method is a very useful tool for positive thinking and I will return to it again in a later chapter. The point to be made now is that it does help to broaden your opening view.

d)   OTHER PEOPLE'S POINTS OF VIEW

It may be useful to consider your problem from somebody else's point of view where this is likely to differ from your own. You

may say to yourself, "What would X do if he were here now?".
You may decide, ultimately to discount this view but its
consideration can be a useful addition to your breadth of
thought.

Apart from "standing in the shoes" of another person, you
may be offered their views direct. Do not dismiss such
comments out of hand. Remember that your own view is limited
both by what you see now, and by your previous experience and
knowledge. Other people, however inexpert, may offer you the
key to a productive line of thought.

e) OBJECTIVES

It can often help to think of the problem in terms of the ultimate
objective. This can lead to totally new methods of approach.
For example, I visited a friend on one occasion, and found him
in the process of extending his burglar alarm system to include
an external boxed bell. He was pondering over the problem of
how to drill a hole through the 14 inch thick wall, when the
longest bit he had for his electric drill was only 6 inches. We
both stood looking up at the outside of his house when I began
to think of the objective. It was not "how to drill a hole through
the wall", it was "how do we connect an electric cable to the
bell?".

I thought of passing the cable through the window or the
wooden sill, but either of these methods would have involved a
vulnerable run of exposed cable. My next thought was to use an
overflow pipe which I could see protruding from the wall. The
cable was thin enough to pass through the pipe without unduly
obstructing it, and was well insulated, against coming into
contact with any water. In any event there would not normally
be a flow of water through the pipe. I suggested the idea to my
friend knowing that he would not be happy with its
imperfections and that he may have dismissed the idea out of
hand. However, he suddenly realised that the pipe had been
made redundant some years previously. We had discovered a
perfect hole in the wall.

CONCLUSION

You may have detected some overlap between these methods
and those described in the previous chapter. For instance the

previous example demonstrates not only the method of looking at the objective, but also the benefits of seeking another person's view, and the difficulties of taking on problems posed by others. There are, however, subtle differences between these methods, and the reason for dealing with them separately is to present as wide a view as possible. The lesson to be drawn from this chapter is "think broadly".

13
THINK IT THROUGH

We are now ready to look at the difficulties which can arise after you have started to work on a problem. Where you are unable to find a satisfactory solution, you should look for an alternative approach. The aim is to overcome the mental blockage by breaking through the thinking structure as illustrated in this diagram:-

Look for ways of breaking through the structure.

PROBLEM

The following seven techniques may be useful in helping you to achieve a breakthrough:-

a) Start again.
b) Examine the structure.
c) Relax the structure.
d) Soften the blocks of the structure.
e) Use imagination.
f) Use chance.
g) Use analogy.

a) START AGAIN. I have already indicated the advantages of adopting a broad opening view of a problem. If this has not been done, and occasionally even if it has, there may be some benefit in starting again and looking for a fresh angle. In the previously mentioned T.V. adventure game (page 35), the late discovery of the buoyancy capability of the plastic bags is a good example of this. Starting again, however, is not easy and will usually be resisted in view of the investment, already made, of time and other resources in reaching the deadlocked position. But, as with the raft, it may be necessary to go back in order to move further forward.

It needs to be emphasised that this "start again" technique should not be used too frequently, and certainly not as an excuse for premature termination of a difficult problem. I have mentioned it here merely to show that it is a direction which may be considered, and should never be totally discounted.

Another reason why this method should be kept in mind as an option, is that the circumstances surrounding a problem may change significantly during its consideration, and earlier decisions may be based on circumstances which no longer prevail.

For example, a proposed new road scheme was planned to cross two railway lines in close proximity to each other. One was a branch line, the other was a siding connection to a cement works. This presented some engineering difficulties because of the need to provide ground level vehicular access between the two new bridges.

In parallel with design works, discussions were held with the users of the siding resulting in a diversion of the siding away from the road line. This removed the need for one of the bridges, but the benefits did not stop there. The repositioning of the siding left the branch line largely redundant and that too was closed, removing the need for the other bridge. The way was now clear for the unimpeded construction of the road. However, using the "start again" principle, the proposed roadline was reviewed, and the plan changed to use the now redundant railway line as the preferred traffic route.

The secret is to keep an open mind and not blank out any possibility of a "start again" movement. I will consider further aspects of this technique later, under the heading "Positive Thinking".

b)   EXAMINE THE STRUCTURE. In an earlier chapter we looked at the way in which the thinking structure is formed out of block patterns, and the dangers of misinterpreting a pattern. In order to ensure that this is not the cause of your mental blockage, it can be beneficial to examine each of the building blocks which make up your thinking structure. You will need to test the assumptions on which they were founded. Try to identify the separate blocks and ask yourself, "was I right to make that assumption, or could there be another explanation?". It is often useful to begin this re-examination by looking at the dominant features, since these carry greatest weight, and tend to blur adequate consideration of the less dominant features. The effect of this is illustrated in this diagram:-

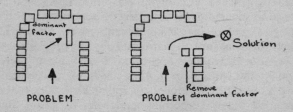

We saw, when looking at magic and humour, how use was made of a dominant idea to mislead and conceal the true position. The reverse of this is to look out for the dominating factors, and then avoid them, or at least temporarily shelve them, while you look at the rest of the structure. In the police search for the Yorkshire Ripper, the dominating factor was a tape recording which was assumed to be the voice of the killer. Because of this, it appears that insufficient weight was attached to other relevant evidence. Indeed, the culprit was interviewed by police on the strength of other evidence, but excluded because of the evidence of the tape. The tape recording was eventually discovered to be a hoax, and irrelevant therefore to the investigation. It is always easy to be wise after the event, but the lesson to be learned is to examine closely each assumption which is made during the thinking exercise.

c)   RELAX THE STRUCTURE.   Try not to be too hidebound by rules, regulations or conventions. They can make the thinking structure very rigid and unduly block your field of search for a solution. Nelson wasn't following rules when he put the telescope to his blind eye. There may be advantages in turning an occasional "blind eye" to circumvent some obstacle. This is particularly so in the development of new ideas where it may be vital to break away from the rules set by previous, failed "experts". They may be prisoners of their own rules, constrained from making any further advance. Accepting their rules may equally constrain you.

I am not advocating total disregard of rules and regulations. I am suggesting that the thinking process be allowed flexibility to experiment and test new ideas with minimum restriction. If this method produces a way forward, then the new information will provide evidence to support your claim that the rules should be changed to accommodate your new theory or practice. It is by using this method that many advances have been made in science. New ideas are often frowned upon by previous experts, and inventors often have to show great resilience to overcome prejudice, and win approval. Alas, this is not always achieved within the inventor's lifetime. The Italian physicist, Avogadro, formulated a law concerning molecules in gases, but the accuracy of his work was not recognised until many years after his death.

d) SOFTEN THE BLOCKS WITHIN THE STRUCTURE. As you get into a problem, it is easy for the constituent blocks which make up the structure to have solid and well defined functions. The more detailed the definition of a block, the less flexibility there will be for change within the structure. Look at this diagram which illustrates the difference between concrete and flexible blocks in the structure:-

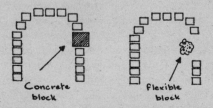

Concrete block

flexible block

This point will be made more clear by reference to examples:-

I once had a steel framed, glass fish tank, which leaked and was beyond repair. I was about to dispose of it when I realised that it would make an ideal garden cloche. While I thought of this object in terms of its name, I had mentally tied up its use for that purpose. As soon as I softened my picture of it, I was able to use it more flexibly.

A friend of mine, leaving a building site, found that his hands were dirty but could not find any water to wash them. He solved his problem by getting me to operate the spray of his car windscreen wash. He was able to unlock this problem by thinking "water" rather than "windscreen wash".

e)   USE IMAGINATION. It is not always necessary to develop your line of thought on a strictly logical and realistic basis. It may be possible to jump over one or two stages in order to overcome some temporary block. This can be done by assuming that the intermediate stages have been overcome even though, for the time being anyway, they have not.

This technique may enable you to discover and develop solid ground beyond the block, which may in turn lead to a solution to your problem. Once the solution has been found, the intermediate stages will either fall into place, or be seen to be unnecessary because an alternative method has been uncovered. The story of the burglar alarm needing a hole in the wall, mentioned earlier, is a good example of this. You will remember that my thought process imagined the electric cable passing through an overflow pipe. Had this pipe still been in use, it would not have been an acceptable passage for the electrics. Nevertheless, we jumped over that problem which enabled us to recognise that the pipe was redundant and provided a perfect solution.

It is, of course, essential to remember which stages have been assumed, so that the stability of the solution can be checked, or alternatively, in the event of deadlock, the hypothesis can be dismantled back to a firm base.

The next diagram illustrates how the thinking process might pass through an obstacle by making an imaginative assumption:-

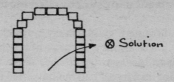

One way to encourage imaginative ideas at the point of an obstacle, is to say to yourself, "Wouldn't it be good if XXXX were to happen?" You may include in your thinking, ideas which may be funny, magic, etc. The aim is to find something which can act as a stepping stone in your thinking process. There will not always be one, but it will not harm to spend some time looking for one, when your way forward is otherwise blocked.

f)   USE CHANCE. There are a number of ways in which chance may introduce some new information to assist your thinking. This information may complete your picture in the same way as finding a missing piece of jig-saw, or may open up an entirely new direction. It will be useful to examine the source of this new information, which may come from some external factor, or arise from an internal reprocessing of existing information.

There may be an occasion when somebody says something, or you casually experience something, which is the key to a solution to a long standing problem. The question on such occasions is whether you recognise the potential of the new information in relation to your problem. Archimedes spotted the solution to his problem when he stepped into his bath. He might easily have missed it. The obstacle is the structure within which the original problem has been considered. If the structure is too tight, then the problem is boxed in, and the potential solution will be passed over, unrecognised. See diagram.

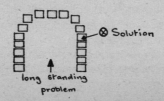

If, on the other hand, you have developed an open, enquiring mind, the structure will be loose, and the new revelation will more easily be recognised as the missing piece of the jig-saw. I shall deal with this in more detail later under the heading "Think yourself lucky", on page 92.

It may be that the missing piece of information is in your mind already, but you have not made the necessary connection. I mentioned in an earlier chapter, how it is possible to store some information in your mind under a particular heading, and for it then to be locked away under that heading. Sometimes you will be aware that you have some vital information hidden away in your mind, but on other occasions it will be totally obscured. There are two main ways in which this hidden information may be retrieved, and I will consider them separately.

Occasionally your subconscious will produce the answer. It is able to do this when your brain is allowed freedom to mull over ideas, unfettered by rigid structures. This is most likely to happen in time of mental relaxation, such as walking in the country, or even during sleep. In the latter case, we can get some idea how the brain operates subconsciously, from recalled dreams. For the purpose of illustration I will mention a dream which a friend recounted to me:-

In his dream, my friend was planning to make a trip abroad and booked to fly, "cottage class". On his arrival at the airport, he entered the living room of a country cottage, and sat in an armchair by the window. The cottage taxied down a main road, and achieved lift off with the aid of a hump back bridge. He began to think that perhaps he should have booked something better than "cottage class", but his main concern was the open fireplace, and particularly the chimney. How was cabin pressure going to be maintained?

The interpretation of dreams is beyond the scope of this book. This example does illustrate, however, how the brain can play with logical and illogical ideas when the structure is relaxed. Sometimes too, there is an element of genius in the absurd – the hump back bridge take-off is not unlike the method used to launch Harrier aircraft from aircraft carriers. Not all subconscious brain activity is revealed in dreams, but the activity carries on just the same. No doubt you have had experience of solutions to problems coming from your subconscious. There is obviously benefit with some problems, therefore, to "sleep on it".

The connection of two pieces of information already stored in your brain, may also occur consciously. I mentioned earlier, the countless number of substructures we can produce, each designed to deal with a particular subject, and each with its own store of locked-in information. These substructures are constantly interrelating as a wide range of thoughts pass through the mind. The use of chance in these cases, is that the newly connected substructure may bring with it the solution to a problem which was previously locked out. See diagram:-

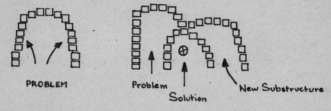

PROBLEM   Problem   New Substructure
                        Solution

Clearly, the number of occasions when information stored in one substructure can help towards a solution in another is somewhat limited, because it relies on the coming together of the two relevant substructures. Archimedes may not have solved his problem if he hadn't taken a bath. A more likely outcome from the cross fertilisation of ideas contained in separate substructures, is the creation of a new idea in a different area altogether. In other words, instead of assisting each other, the two substructures combine to produce a third, new substructure.

I mentioned earlier that a common link can be found between almost any two substructures. Clearly, these links will not all be capable of being developed profitably, but there is obviously an infinite number of possible combinations, and consequently, lots of opportunities for new ideas. For example, consider the combination of the hovercraft with the lawnmower. The hover mower is not so much an improvement of the lawnmower, it is more a diversification. Both have their relative advantages and disadvantages which provide plenty of scope for the manufacturers in their battle for market supremacy. The invention has, in fact, widened the range of garden work which can now be assisted mechanically. The exciting feature of the hover mower is the dual function of the rotor arm, which not only carries the cutting edge, but also the fan which develops the floating cushion of air.

There is obviously a connection between these two types of mower, but it does not necessarily follow that there needs to be such a close link in order to develop a new idea. Opportunities may arise to move into a new area altogether. For example, imagine a problem of a draughty room. Attempts may be made to identify, and seal, inlets. If this is not successful, then attention may be switched to trying to stop air passing OUT of the room. (This technique will be considered in more detail in the next chapter.) Further investigation may lead to consideration of the differences in air pressure inside and outside the room. Next may be a thought that the draught could be eliminated by ensuring that the air pressure within the room was greater than that immediately outside. This could lead to an interest in pressurising rooms, which in turn, could lead to the invention of the pressurised domes used in fairgrounds and open exhibitions. The initial problem of the draughty room has been shelved, while the idea of the pressurised dome has changed the direction of thought into an entirely new area.

In order to capitalise on instances of chance, you should develop an open, enquiring mind. It is also important to look at things loosely, so that you can assess the potential for an object to perform beyond the limits assigned to it in a tightly structured context. You should also adopt a flexible approach, and be prepared to change direction if a new opportunity presents itself.

g) USE ANALOGY. Analogies are often used as a means of describing to another person, some aspect of a particular subject by reference to a parallel case. They can provide a useful and picturesque way of looking at one subject in terms of another, but they should be used with care because they can never be totally accurate. The degree to which comparisons can be extended will differ from case to case, but over-extension will inevitably lead to inaccuracy. Provided you are aware of these limitations, the use of analogy can provide a valuable means of developing an idea.

For example, in Chapter 1, I used the analogy of breathing to describe what I wanted to say about thinking. When I first selected this analogy my aim was to describe the spontaneity of the process, but as I considered it further, I began to look at differing standards of performance, and the opportunity for improvement by training. The use of this analogy enabled me to ask questions about the subject which I might not otherwise have covered. I conveniently overlooked the fact that breathing is itself controlled by the thinking process with which I was trying to draw comparison.

The benefits to be gained by using analogies can be illustrated diagramatically as follows:-

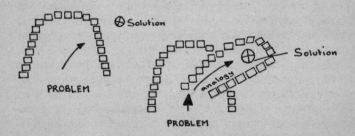

The analogy has its own structure which is superimposed onto the structure of the main subject, forming a window. If the view through this window reveals something which is relevant to the main subject, then the new information will quickly be drawn into the main structure.

CONCLUSION

All the methods described in this chapter are designed to help you see beyond the structure in your search for a solution to a problem. As we have seen previously, the structure itself discourages this wider search. There is, of course, no guarantee of a successful outcome, but your opportunity for success is considerably enhanced. If and when an external solution is found, it will be taken into the structure, where it will be recognised as quite normal. Indeed, you will probably wonder why you did not think of the solution earlier.

14
INVERTED THINKING

If the hill will not come to Mahomet, Mahomet will go to the hill. Within this well known statement lies the key to the solution to many problems. It is a further technique for avoiding the restrictions of structured thinking. Quite simply the method is to turn the problem upside down, inside out, or back to front. This is inverted thinking.

You will be familiar with the type of children's picture puzzle which requires you to identify which, of a number of anglers, has caught the only fish which is attached to one of their entangled lines. You may have to trace the line of every individual angler before you discover which one has the fish. Clearly, however, the problem is made much easier if the line is traced from the fish to the successful angler.

Similarly when planning a route for travel, it may be planned from A. to B., or alternatively, from B. to A.

In these two examples, the opportunity to invert the approach was obvious, because the entire problem, and solution, were both visible. The method may be equally appropriate, however, even where the solution is not visible at the outset. Police detective work is a good example of this. They often tackle the problem from both ends simultaneously. On one hand, they start at the scene of the crime, collecting evidence in pursuit of the culprit. On the other, they assess known villains to see if they match the details of the particular crime. In the first case they ask "who did it?", in the second they ask "was it Mr. X?". The difficulty, of course, is knowing where to start the search for Mr. X.

Similarly, the difficulty of using this method for general

problem solving, is defining the limit of search for the missing piece of information. Often a system of trial and error has to be adopted.

There are other, more easily defined, methods of using inverted thinking to provide a breakthrough. These may relate to whole problems, or some constituent element, and are best described by reference to specific examples:-

a) A father of a young toddler, unable to get five minutes peace to read his newspaper, sat inside the child's playpen, allowing the child the freedom of the room. The playpen is designed to keep a child in, it can also be used to keep him out. This must have other uses beside the one just mentioned.

b) The best form of defence is attack.

c) I once ordered too much wet mix concrete for a particular job and had some surplus. My neighbour advised me to remove the surplus before it hardened, and suggested that we placed it in small heaps on a polythene sheet for easy disposal later. After they had hardened, I picked up the first one to throw it away, and realised that it had a perfectly smooth base. I turned it over so that the flat side was uppermost, and laid it, together with the others, as stepping stones across my lawn.

d) You will have read stories of upturned boats being used as human shelters.

e) I also mentioned the problem of the draughty room. Instead of stopping air coming into the room, efforts were switched to stopping it getting out. Most people, faced with a draughty room, would probably attempt to seal the draught from inside, when it may be easier to seal it from the outside.

f) Returning from a caravan holiday one wet afternoon, we passed a caravan travelling in the opposite direction. I expressed my concern for the poor people going on holiday on a rainy day, but was corrected by my young daughter who said "They could be going home too".

g) On a beach in the south of France sat a man in business clothes, with a briefcase by his side and a string of coloured pens tied round his neck. I watched, as he worked through his papers oblivious to the topless bathing beauties sitting all around. I thought him stupid for bringing his work with him on holiday, but then wondered whether he was, in fact, a local businessman relaxing during normal working hours.

h) A man was stopped by security men as he left the docks pushing a wheelbarrow full of odds and ends. After a thorough inspection, he was allowed to continue. Next day, he appeared again with a similar load which passed inspection. This continued for a few weeks, until the routine became very familiar to the gate inspector. He suspected something, but could not put his finger on it. Eventually, it turned out that the man had been stealing wheelbarrows.

i) If a screw cannot be removed from woodwork because it is in too tight, it can usually be loosened by tightening it a little further first.

The important feature of this technique is that it enables you to approach a problem from another direction. This may help you to solve your problem, or may prevent you from jumping to incorrect conclusions as illustrated in some of these examples. Alternatively, it may open up something entirely new. In any event you should find the method very useful from time to time.

15
KEEP THINKING

Up to this point, it has been assumed that the thinking process is concerned mainly with handling self-contained, identifiable problems. In practice, however, mental activity is far more complex.

The brain is a control centre which has to receive, store, process and transmit, masses of information affecting each individual's physical, emotional, social, environmental and intellectual well-being. In order to achieve this, the brain frequently changes from one subject to another, often handling a number of subjects simultaneously. Contrast that with a computer which is programmed to carry out particular tasks, and allowed uninterrupted time to complete them. Clearly, the computer can perform these particular tasks far more quickly and accurately than a human brain, but the brain is vastly superior in its depth and range. This enables it to cross-fertilize ideas so that variations to the norm can be dealt with, and totally new ideas can be developed.

The techniques we have looked at to open up the structure of individual problems are equally relevant to the complex brain activity I have just described. Perhaps the benefits can now be seen more clearly. Given that so much information passes through the brain, there is obvious merit in reducing the blockages which restrict the free use of that information. If the information is there, it is a waste not to use it. It may not surface very readily, but as you keep thinking, so the likelihood of successful retrieval is increased.

You will recall that, although a great number of black and white problems have a single correct answer, a major part of our thinking is concerned with grey matters, for which there may be many different answers. The perfect, or elegant, solution in these cases may well be a matter of personal preference. The diagrams used up to now have indicated a single solution, whereas there may be a number of potential solutions. See diagrams:-

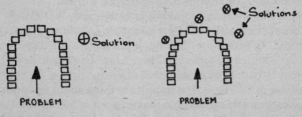

Single solution   Numerous solutions

There may, of course, be a solution within the structure, in which case it is likely to be found relatively easily. Likewise, if one of the external solutions is discovered, it will be quickly swallowed up in a new structure. See diagrams:-

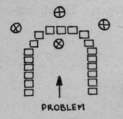 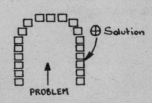

Solution within structure   External solution discovered

In any event, the discovery of a solution is likely to end any further search. There will certainly not be a lot of enthusiasm for continued effort. This phenomenon is probably the largest block to be overcome in breaking out of structured thinking, and understandably so. The difficulty lies in seeing why you should give up, or pass over, something concrete and acceptable in order to search for something else which may not even exist. Even if a second solution is found, should the search continue for a third, and so on? It is easier to settle for the "bird in the hand", but mankind would stagnate if this principle were applied universally. We must continue to look for new answers.

To use an analogy of space exploration, we lift off from our problem (earth) and head for a visible objective, (the moon). On arrival, we can say, "Good. This is it", or we can set out again for one of the planets. On achieving that, we can call a halt, or press on into the unknown, in search of Utopia.

So far as everyday thinking is concerned, it is clearly not practical continually to reject adequate solutions, in search of an ideal. As with most thinking, it is a matter of balance which has to be settled subjectively. There has to be a cut off point, and there may have to be some compromise in terms of the solution available at that time. The important thing about this principle is to recognise its existence so that an open mind can be retained at all times. In this way, you will be able to make positive decisions on the basis of the best available solution, whilst remaining receptive to new ideas.

The kite has been flown very successfully for many years on a single string. The introduction of a second string revolutionised it, literally. There are countless other examples of progress beyond the merely acceptable. It is exciting and challenging to think that there is no limit to this progress. The all important thing is to *Keep thinking*.

PART III

INTRODUCTION

We have now looked at the advantages and disadvantages of structured thinking, and the numerous methods of overcoming mental blockage to help problem solving and open up new opportunities. In this next part of the book, the aim is to look at some of the practical applications of these thinking processes and consider how they can be put to personal advantage. For example, how can you programme yourself to be more successful? How can positive thinking give you better personal control?

Although the thinking process is very personal, it does not operate in a vacuum. It is influenced greatly by the way other people think and behave. Communication and contact may involve conflict or co-operation, and this may lead to consensus or compromise. Group allegiances, status, and emotions all play their part in influencing this thinking, and to understand them is therefore vital, both personally, and to any manager who seeks to optimise the efficiency and effectiveness of human resources. All these matters are considered in some detail.

No investigation of the thinking process would be complete without some consideration being given to *memory* which is, after all, the central store of information on which the whole process relies. In the final chapter, therefore, I have attempted to identify the natural strengths and weaknesses of memory, in order to use them to develop techniques which can be used to improve individual memory power.

16
THINK BIKE

In a recent road-safety advert on the television, attention was focused on the need for motorists to be particularly watchful for motor-cyclists at road junctions. Accident figures had shown that motor-cyclists were especially vulnerable at T-junctions, where other motor vehicles turned onto the major road across their path. The advert showed an example of a typical accident, and then emphasised the need for motorists to "Think Bike". The message was simple, and the frequent repetition was designed to make it stick in the minds of all motorists.

In the chapter headed "Think Straight", we looked at high probability, structured thinking, and the way in which it enables us to think quickly with economy of effort. In some cases, mental effort can be reduced to an absolute minimum by making a deliberately deep imprint on the mind. This is the method used to implant the multiplication tables in the minds of young school children. Once the tables have been mastered, the information may be retrieved instantly at any time. For example, what does $7 \times 9 = ?$ How do you know? The answer is that you just know. You don't have to perform a mathematical calculation in your head to produce the answer. You are programmed to produce an instant answer.

Incidentally, in a recent discussion programme on the radio, an educationist explained that modern teaching of multiplication is based more on understanding, than knowledge. The children are taught to work out for themselves, that if, for example, six of them have three items each, then collectively they have eighteen. This may be all that is required in the days of the electronic calculator, but it will not enable the children to produce an instant answer in their heads.

In the case of the road safety slogan, the aim was for the information to surface automatically at the appropriate time, the trigger for this recall being the motorist's arrival at a road junction.

Ideas and emotions can also be imprinted on the brain to produce a "mind-set", or fixation. These can result from particular personal experiences, which resurface automatically, each time a similar set of circumstances is encountered. They may be positive or negative, and can be a major source of continued stress. The mind begins to believe that the individual is under threat and will not be able to cope successfully, even though the experience which gave rise to the feeling may have been untypical. For example, if you met a foreigner who was particularly unpleasant to you, you may feel that all people of that nationality are going to be similarly unpleasant. This may influence your behaviour to them, which may draw the unpleasant reaction, and you will then claim that your original feelings were justified.

If you are able to identify these "mind-sets", you may try to rationalise them in a quieter moment and reprogramme yourself to react differently in future.

It may be that the "mind-set" has developed over a long period and is out of date. We all get involved in some routine and there is nothing wrong with that. Routine can be very comfortable and requires minimum effort. The danger is however that it becomes so automatic, we stop questioning whether our actions are still relevent or could be bettered.

Mind-sets are not necessarily restricted to an individual, and may be held in common with large sections of the population. For example, some men regard women as bad drivers. Actually there is no statistical evidence for this view, although isolated examples will be claimed to prove the rule. Try to think of other commonly held mind-sets and ask yourself whether, in your experience, they are capable of being sustained.

Up to this point, the mind-sets we have considered have been of a permanent, or semi-permanent, character. They may also arise in the short term such as during consideration of a problem. I have already mentioned how a dominant idea may obscure a possible solution. It is possible for this dominant idea to become a mind-set, so that it is treated as a concrete fact and no longer questioned. The solution will never be found so long as this mind-set holds. Alternatively, it can just get in the way of normal every-day activities.

Mind-sets can also be used positively. I have cultivated an unemotional response to the idiotic speed merchants who overtake me precariously on the road. I could get very heated and try to redress the score, but I don't. Instead, I imagine that they have some particularly urgent business to attend to, such as an emergency at the hospital, and wish them God speed.

THINK YOURSELF LUCKY

This positive use of mind-sets can lead you to good fortune in a number of ways:-

1) *Attitude*. You may programme yourself to look at life optimistically. Problems are very rarely as bad as they may appear at the outset, and adopting an optimistic approach may mean the difference between success and failure. I will have more to say about this in Chapter 18 on "positive thinking".

2) *Looking on the bright side*. If you are stuck with a particular problem, try to find something good about it. For example, if it rains on a day when you could have done without it, don't waste your time moaning about it, think instead about what you can do, or, alternatively, enjoy getting wet. You can also think about the benefits of rain, to the garden etc. and you will have a measure to judge the sunnier days.

3) *Make your own luck*. Some years ago, I discovered the benefit of using a mind-set on the football field. A late interception denied my making contact with a flying header at goal. I lay on the ground for a moment, picturing in my mind the goal that I might have scored. While I was lying there, the ball hit the crossbar and dropped in front of me, but I was not quick enough to take advantage. After that experience, I programmed myself to imagine that every shot on goal was going to hit the woodwork and rebound into play, or alternatively, that shots at the goalkeeper were going to be dropped. This simple reprogramming proved very successful. Ninety-five per cent of the time, the anticipated occurrence did

not happen, but when it did, I was ready, and usually the defence was not. I began to score many more goals, the majority of which were regarded as "lucky" or "opportunist". In these situations, however, you make your own luck.

The same principle can be used when driving a car. I was always told to imagine that the other road users were stupid, and capable of breaking the highway code at any time. This programming of the mind teaches you not to take any traffic movements for granted, and leaves space for you to anticipate the "unexpected".

4)   *Believe in success*. Returning to sport, there is evidence to show that individual performances can be improved by programming the mind to believe in success. In golf, for example, it is better to imagine your shot finishing up where you want it, rather than worrying that it might finish up somewhere else. And in high jumping, you may have seen athletes rehearsing in their minds, every step of their run up and the jump. Salesmen must believe they are going to be successful in order to help them overcome the disappointments of their inevitable failures.

The conclusion to be drawn from this chapter is to be aware of mind-sets, and use them to your advantage, rather than allowing them to rule you. And why not read again, the poem on page 11?

17
THINK TANK

When a group of people pool their thoughts with a view to producing a collective answer, the group is often referred to as a "think tank". The obvious benefit of such a gathering, is that the total range of knowledge and experience is much broader than that of any of the individual group members.

This is illustrated in general terms in this diagram.

THINK TANK RANGE

In practice, there is likely to be some duplication, or overlap, as shown in this diagram.

THINK TANK RANGE

There are, however, other benefits of the think tank, as well as a number of potential pitfalls which need to be looked at more closely.

Ideally, there should be a free flow of ideas between the members of the group. The attraction of this is that each individual will receive new information from the other members. In each case, the person who provides the information may have exhausted his use of it, or not realised its full potential. On the other hand, the persons receiving the information may have their eyes opened in the manner described earlier when we considered the effects of breaking through structured thinking.

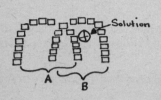

In these diagrams, B. has some information which is locked into his structured thinking. The information is outside A's structured thinking, but when it is revealed to him, he is able to combine it with his own knowledge and experience to produce a new idea which was previously unrecognised by B.

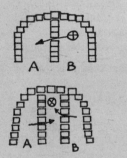

The whole information lies within the new combined A.B. structure.

There may also be cases where an exchange of ideas leads to a discovery which was previously outside the knowledge and experience of any of the group members.

The main pitfall to be avoided is the reverse of the process just considered. Instead of allowing new information to be used by other members of the group, the "owner" of the information claims "expert" control over it, and blocks attempts by others to develop it. Referring to the earlier diagrams, the danger is that B. will not be able to make any further use of his information, and will deny A. an opportunity to discover a breakthrough in B.'s protected territory. This problem can easily arise in a group comprised of mixed professional disciplines, or where senior members dominate the group.

PRINCIPLES FOR CO-OPERATION

In order to overcome these pitfalls and to obtain maximum thinking potential for the group, the following principles should be followed:-

1) Individuals should encourage each others' new lines of thought. It is often better to extend and broaden an idea, rather than block it. Blocking is too easy, is negative, does not help the group, and should be avoided as much as possible.

2) Experts should avoid taking an arrogant stance, and should be receptive to suggestions made by the rest of the group.

3) Individuals should be encouraged to contribute fully without fear of ridicule or rejection.

4) If an individual's idea is rejected by the group, he should attempt to bounce back with new ideas, or at least support some of the others. He should not opt out. It is the idea which is rejected – not the individual. Other members should keep a watchful eye and attempt to remotivate anyone who drops out in this manner.

5) Individuals who feel that an acceptable solution has been obtained, should nevertheless continue to support and encourage the group in its search for something better.

The aim must be to make full use of all the mental resources within the group. Each member should adopt a flexible open mind and be supportive of the other members.

18
POSITIVE THINKING

"He who hesitates is lost", and "Make hay while the sun shines", are two well known proverbs which may be said to support the idea of positive thinking. Unfortunately, however, it is not as simple as that. I have already drawn attention to the dangers of jumping to incorrect conclusions, and suggested that the remedy is to adopt a more cautious approach. This may also be supported by a number of proverbs: "Fools rush in where angels fear to tread"; "More haste – less speed"; and "Look before you leap".

Proverbs are expressions of well known truths, and yet the second group clearly contradicts the first. How can they all be right? The answer is that it depends on the circumstances. There will be occasions when speed is essential, and others when thorough preparation is vital.

We are, therefore, faced with two extremes; on the one hand, making impulsive decisions with reckless abandon; and on the other, putting off making decisions until there is a prior guarantee of success. Somewhere between these two positions, lies the role of positive thinking, which requires thoughtful preparation and committed execution.

CHARACTERISTICS OF POSITIVE THINKING
The attitude of a positive thinker should be forward looking, optimistic and resilient. The benefits of adopting these characteristics can be illustrated in the form of the diagrams used throughout this book:-

1. *Negative structured
    thinking*.
Thinking is generally
pessimistic and
difficulties are seen as
major obstacles which
are avoided rather than
tackled. This creates an
artificial barrier which
reduces the thinking
capacity of the
structure.

2. *Positive structured
    thinking*.
Difficulties are seen as
hurdles rather than
barriers, and full use is
made of the thinking
structure which
increases opportunity
for success.

3. *Extended positive
    thinking*.
Full use is made of the
structure, and efforts
are made to secure a
breakthrough by
extending beyond the
structure as described
earlier in this book.
Opportunities for
success are maximised.

Throughout this book, we have been looking at the thinking
process in terms of problem solving. Although part of our
thinking is involved with specifically identified problems, much
of it is directed towards normal, everyday routine. Often we
deal with two or three different matters at the same time, and by

the end of a day we will have processed hundreds of separate topics and activities. Some of these will have been processed spontaneously, in an instant, while others will have been constructed over a longer period. To make things more difficult, our brains will have switched attention from one subject to another, partly under self control, but also in a haphazard manner. Haphazard switching presents its own difficulties, and I will return to this subject later.

Individuals themselves largely control their own levels of mental effort and stimulation. Some people choose to be active and positive, while others prefer to be more passive. It is not necessary to be totally one or the other. Provided the characteristics of positive thinking are known, it should be possible to switch it on or off, to suit individual convenience. In this sense it may be likened to driving a car. The accelerator pedal is available to inject more speed and power, but it is not necessary, or even good, to drive on full power all the time.

There are five aspects to consider:

1) Degree of energy needed to complete exercise.

2) Personal ambition and ability.

3) Need for action.

4) Positive thinking techniques.

5) Acceptance.

1) DEGREE OF ENERGY REQUIRED

Every action we take is preceded by a conscious, or subconscious, thought. The degree of energy needed to convert it into action ranges from spontaneous intuition, such as scratching your nose, to substantial conscious effort, such as writing a book, or developing a new product. In this latter case, the solution, or result, will have to be constructed. It will be necessary to identify the project, and determine the required plan of action. This, in itself, will not solve the problem. Physical and mental effort will be needed to convert the plan into action. Other, subsidiary, problems will have to be overcome, such as availability of time, equipment, finance, and skill. Ultimate success will depend, among other things, on your attitude of approach, and characteristics such as resilience, resourcefulness, perseverence and patience.

As each problem is different, so too will be the amount of energy required for conversion to a satisfactory conclusion. In addition, there are differences between individuals. In view of this, it is not possible to draw hard and fast rules. It is largely a question of personal choice whether an individual wishes to adopt a positive approach or not. The significance of this choice, and the ability to recognise it, will become more clear later in this chapter.

2)   AMBITION AND ABILITY

Clearly, no system of thinking can guarantee a successful outcome in terms of obtaining a solution to a problem, or achieving an objective. The ratio of success to failure differs between individuals and is influenced by current levels of ambition and ability. Consider the relationship between these characteristics with the following three individuals:-

a)   This person is over-ambitious and is likely to experience a relatively high failure rate. In the longer term, ability may catch up with ambition, but the danger is that ambition will fade due to the disheartenment of frequent failure.

> AMBITION
> ABILITY

b)   This person is more balanced and likely to have fewer failures. Ambition is sufficiently ahead to encourage an extension of ability.

> AMBITION
> ABILITY

c)   This person is very unambitious. Failure rate is likely to be low because difficult problems will be avoided. Achievement will also be low because of the lack of ambition.

> AMBITION
> ABILITY

The purpose of this illustration is to indicate how positive thinking can help different people in different ways. In the first place, it encourages individuals to relate ambition more realistically to ability. This will beneficially extend the unambitious, and curb the excesses of wishful thinkers. Secondly it encourages action, which extends experience and leads to improved ability.

I should emphasise that the aim of positive thinking is not to curb realistic ambitions. Ambition is the main driving force. I have already given examples of people achieving the so-called impossible, having been driven on by a personal ambition. The aim here, is to draw your attention to these characteristics so that you can recognise them, and hopefully control their level of influence on your current thinking. The relevance of this personal control will be seen later in this chapter.

3) NEED FOR ACTION

The freedom of choice to decide whether or not to adopt positive thinking differs from time to time and depends upon the degree of urgency attached to the particular issue. In order to consider this choice of approach more fully, it will be useful to catagorise the need for action into four levels of urgency, as follows:-

i) *Urgent and Critical*.

These are the problems which confront everybody from time to time, and have to be overcome in order to maintain status quo, or minimise regression. In its most basic form it may be a matter of survival, which will usually stir even the most negative thinkers. For example, you might be in a building which suddenly catches fire. Clearly, these problems are not overcome without some effort, but the severity of the situation is usually sufficient motivation to encourage positive action.

ii) *Important but not Pressing*.

This is where the first real opportunity for choice arises. Positive thinkers will tackle these problems at the earliest opportunity, whereas negative people will defer taking action for as long as possible. You may have heard about the man who had a hole in the roof of his house. When it was raining, it was too wet to get

on the roof to mend it, and when it was dry, the roof did not
need mending. Problems of this nature, which manifest
themselves spasmodically, should be attended to during the
quieter moments between crises. The need for action may not be
visible during these periods, and so an element of positive
thinking will be required to identify and deal with it before the
next crisis.

iii) *Avoidable*.

Problems may be avoided so long as they do not cause personal
discomfort, although sometimes even this will not stir a
negative thinker into action. If the discomfort is not too great, it
is possible to adjust your thinking to accept the imperfections as
normal. Whether in your business or personal life, you can
probably make your own extensive list of jobs which could be
done, or alternatively which you can avoid. Maybe you have
been avoiding some of them for a long time.

It may be that some problems are avoidable now, but will
inevitably become critical in due course. For example,
maintenance jobs can often be deferred for a time. In recent
years, because of financial constraints, schools and highways
maintenance programmes were severely cut back. The saving is
only temporary, and because of escalating deterioration, often
ends in a far more expensive job having to be done. Sometimes,
of course, there is merit in delaying a maintenance job, if other
elements of the fabric are obsolescent. Each case has to be
treated according to its merits. The important thing is to make
the right decision, and be prepared to follow through.

From the positive thinking point of view, it may be useful to
analyse each avoidable problem, in order to assess the
cost/benefit consequences of taking immediate, delayed, or no
action. It may be, of course, that there are many such problems
waiting to be tackled, in which event some ranking of priority
will be necessary. I will return shortly to the difficulties of
having to cope with a large number of problems concurrently.

iv) *Routine*.

These are the normal everyday activities which provide greatest
scope for positive thinking because they do not demand
immediate or urgent attention. The brain is therefore free to

develop its own priorities, and will benefit from the increased mental activity involved. This can be achieved in a number of ways which are to be dealt with next.

4) POSITIVE THINKING TECHNIQUES
i) *Setting Objectives.*

We saw earlier in this chapter, how we may be encouraged to deal with urgent and critical matters. The aim here, is to set an objective, and treat it with the same degree of importance. Anybody can set themselves an objective, or target. For example, learning a new skill, saving to buy something, planning to make something. Very often the objective will include a timescale within which it is to be achieved. Setting an objective is very like defining a problem, in the sense that they both require an input of effort, and ultimate success is not guaranteed.

Targets should be set realistically, and should be reasonably attainable, although some degree of risk may be taken. (I will have more to say about risk, later). Overambitious targets may be no more than a wishful dream or fantasy, and for this reason should be avoided. Once set, the objective should be pursued with commitment which may be made as a personal resolution, may be declared to another person, or based on some financial or other stake.

ii) *Proactivity.*

Being proactive means thinking ahead, so that plans can be made to cope with, or even direct, future events. It is fire prevention, rather than fire fighting. We have already seen how structured thinking enables us to react quickly in familiar circumstances, by recalling previous experiences. This process works very successfully in the majority of cases, but relies on external factors remaining fairly constant, and therefore predictable. If and when circumstances change, it will be necessary to identify the change and adjust the structure accordingly. There is likely to be some delay in reaction time during this adjustment period, with a consequent loss of some control. If the change can be foreseen, then there is obvious benefit in planning ahead, rather than waiting to be overtaken by events.

In a provincial town recently, a cycle and pram dealer decided that the major part of his business, cycles, would benefit from a move to the edge of the town, away from the pedestrianised centre. He calculated that the pram side of the business could cope with this move. The business was relocated accordingly, and the proprietor was pleasantly surprised to find that, not only did the cycle business flourish, but the pram sales rocketed, to the extent that they became the major part of the business. The reason for this was the on-site car park which the new premises enjoyed, and which was a God-send for expectant mums.

The point about this example is that the business had obviously changed over a prolonged period. It was continuing to survive in its town centre location, and the proprietor could be forgiven for not recognising the effects of the change in external circumstances. In the event, he made himself time for some proactive thinking, and benefited from his willingness to take positive action.

There are many new developments in high technology to which some people adapt very quickly, while others are reluctant to give them a try. In the main, it is the younger people who are most receptive to new ideas, the reason being that they are still developing a thinking structure and are keen to learn from new experiences. Older people, on the other hand, have well established mental structures and tend to prefer the familiar, rather than involve themselves in the risk and effort of exploring new territory.

Whether you are young or old, the choice is yours. You may apply proactive thinking in your business or personal life. Ask yourself such questions as: "How can I improve my product to satisfy future demand and stay ahead of my competitors?", or "Where am I going and what do I want to achieve?". In each case the method is to identify possible trends and ask yourself what you should be doing about it. You may even decide to take control and actually set the new trend. This is what "Golden Wonder" did when they entered the potato crisp market in the UK, hitherto dominated by Smiths. They decided to take their crisps into supermarkets and aimed their sales at the housewife and children. This in turn led to the introduction of flavoured crisps and other snack foods. During this time, "Smiths" experienced increased sales, but their share of the market fell sharply.

You should always try to make some time for proactive thinking. Remember that fire prevention reduces the need for fire fighting, and is much less painful.

iii) *Mind set.*

In chapter 16, "Think Bike", we looked at ways in which the brain can be programmed to react in a particular way. The same method can be used to promote a confident attitude. For example, you may repeat to yourself such phrases as: "Every day in every way, I get better and better", or "I can and I will". Similarly you may condition the way you see things: a bottle of wine may be considered half full rather than half empty. Complex problems can and should be approached on the basis that they *can* be resolved once intervening hurdles have been overcome; rather than that they *cannot* be resolved because of apparent insurmountable barriers. Attitude of approach can be the difference between success and failure. More often than not, problems diminish in severity as they are tackled, and in this way can be likened to an approaching steep hill which always looks worse from a distance but appears to flatten out the nearer one gets to it.

iv) *F.A.N.*

I have already referred to the method of analysing problems by listing separately, the features which are FOR, AGAINST, or NEUTRAL (F.A.N.). Taking these in turn:-

FOR. It is likely that the advantages, or benefits, listed in this column will be attractive in their own right, and will not need any special attention to motivate action. However, be prepared for this list to be increased.

AGAINST. I have already said that items in this column should be regarded as hurdles rather than barriers, but there is another method which may be used to reduce or overturn the disadvantage. To do this it is necessary to examine each apparent disadvantage and look for something good about it. Most difficulties are not so bad that they do not have something good about them. Remember, "every cloud has a silver lining".

The principle underlying this method is that good points are often obscured by a dominant disadvantage. The mental structure focuses on the disadvantage, and blocks out the search for anything better. Part II of this book dealt with the methods of overcoming this, and will aid your careful consideration of each item in this list.

Any advantages that you may be able to identify in this way, should be added to your FOR column, even though they may be relatively less important than the dominant disadvantage. It may even be possible to turn the problem round so that the apparent difficulty becomes a positive benefit. For example, I mentioned earlier the proposal for a new road to cross a railway, and how an apparent difficulty was overcome by the closure of the line. The new road was then constructed along the former railway track, so that the cause of the original problem, finally became the solution.

NEUTRALS. These are the consequences of the main problem which neither support nor oppose it. Careful examination of each of these may reveal some benefit which may then be added to the FOR column. In particular, opportunities for advantageous duplication may present themselves, i.e. try killing two birds with one stone. The duplicate action may not aid the solution of the particular problem, but the benefits may be sufficient to swing the overall balance into favour. Remember, the aim of this method is to look for ways of tackling a problem rather than reasons for not doing so.

v) *Excessive Workload.*
"Having too much to do" is often used as an excuse for doing nothing. Dealing with a large amount of work is certainly a problem, and one which requires a positive approach.

It has been said that if you want someone to do a job, you should ask a busy person. This is not as stupid as it might appear, and is often proved to be true in practice. A number of conclusions can be drawn from this which can help to promote a positive attitude.

Firstly, being active produces a momentum effect, such that the energy developed to deal with one activity is carried through to the next. This principle may be put to good effect when you are faced with a large number of jobs. Instead of worrying about the size of the overall task, or order of priority, the key is to make a start on any one of the jobs. Adjustments to take account of priorities can be made later, once the positive attitude has been developed. This principle applies equally to very large tasks, which often look less daunting once they have been started. Tackling these may be made easier if they can be fragmented and dealt with as a number of smaller problems.

Secondly, it often does not help to get too involved in any particular problem. Your ideas may become too subjective, or emotional, and certain features may become over-dominant. This may be avoided if you have other activities, or problems, to switch attention to occasionally. When you return to the original problem, your view will be more objective, and your subconscious may have moved you closer to a solution. The conclusion to be drawn from this is that if you feel overwhelmed with problems, it may be better to take on more activities, rather than less. Clearly, this is a matter of balance which must be decided by the individual.

vi) *Switching Attention.*
One of the difficulties of trying to cope with a large number of tasks is dealing with the inevitable interruptions. This switching of attention from one subject to another may be deliberate and controlled, and may be used as a means of stepping away from a demanding, or deadlocked, problem. If, and when, you choose to do this, it will be helpful if you prefix the moment when you will return to the problem.

External interruptions are another matter altogether. They can be very frustrating, and have an adverse effect on performance. For this reason, every effort should be made to avoid unnecessary interruptions, although you will never eliminate them altogether. It is what happens AFTER an interruption that is most important in terms of being positive.

If the interrupted task is one requiring physical rather than mental effort, it will be relatively easy to resume. If, on the other hand, the task requires considerable mental effort, the unwelcome interruption will create a tension which will tighten up the thinking structure, and make it difficult to resume effectively. When this happens, it is better not to return immediately to the interrupted task. Switch instead, to a job requiring more physical effort as this will benefit from the extra energy generated by the frustration, and will allow time for the thinking structure to relax. If you haven't any physical jobs to switch to, then making a cup of tea, or taking a short walk will have the same beneficial effect.

vii) *Risk*.

Sometimes the excuse for lack of action is uncertainty of outcome. Although this may be justified in some cases, it should not become the accepted rule. There will be occasions when it is necessary to take some degree of risk in order to make progress. If possible, it is advisable to assess the nature and extent of the risk at the outset. One approach is to consider the worst possible outcome, and measure the risk against that. This may indicate some unpleasantness, cost, or inconvenience, but may not necessarily be catastrophic. Such risks may be worth taking.

Another method is to make the decision to proceed first, and then work to prove that the decision was right. I said earlier, that being right is often a matter for subjective assessment. In these cases, the only risk is one of continued confidence and commitment to make it work. For example, some years ago I decided to tow our caravan to the south of France for one of our holidays. There were two ways I could have arrived at this decision. The first, was to analyse all the possible problems, and make sure each was covered before finalising the arrangements. The second, was to make a definitive decision to go, and then deal with the consequential problems as they arose. I opted for the second method and did have to face a number of problems. Had I chosen the first method, I might not have reached the point of deciding to go. In the event, we had an enjoyable and successful holiday.

One other form of risk involves the investment of time or other resource on a project, when there is no guarantee of ultimate success, and a near miss is failure. Many research projects come into this category. They are normally financed from other profitable activities, and are justified by the rewards which success would bring. Individuals will not have the luxury of this form of cover, and may have to underwrite the risk themselves.

Some time ago, there was a competition on T.V. requiring a sentence, or story, to be composed of words beginning with each consequetive letter of the alphabet. I started by referring to the biblical story, "A boy called David", and continued, with the aid of a dictionary, "effectively fought Goliath. Heavenly inspired juvenile killer launched missile, nullifying outsize Philistine's quality regimental stance. The unbeatable, vanquished, . . .". It was three hours since I had started, and I had only W.X.Y.Z. to go. I had enjoyed the exercise to this point, but did not hold any great hope of being able to satisfy the final, most difficult letters. I searched through the dictionary under X, and came to "xenophobia", meaning "dislike, or fear of foreigners". Not only did this word fit – it was precisely in line with the subject of my story, which I was now able to complete, ". . . with xenophobic youthful zeal". My investment in time had paid off, but it may just as easily have failed. The story would not have been written, had I not been prepared to risk my time.

5) ACCEPTANCE

Positive thinking is not just a matter of driving yourself forward and overcoming any obstacles that get in your way. Sometimes, the obstacles are, in fact, barriers which must be looked at realistically. There is no benefit in lamenting things that have gone wrong, or wishing that things were not what they are. We all experience these types of problems; a damaged car; a broken arm; a failed exam; a lost possession, etc. The list is endless. Don't waste mental energy on wishful thinking. The sooner you accept the realistic view, the sooner you will be able to focus attention on a current problem. By all means look for any lessons that might be learned for the future, but concentrate your current thinking on the state of affairs as they really are.

This advice is expressed very clearly in the positive thinker's prayer:-

God grant me the courage to change the things which need to be changed.

The grace to accept the things which cannot.

And the wisdom to be able to distinguish.

19

THAT'S WHAT YOU THINK.

1. KNOWLEDGE AND EXPERIENCE

In chapter 4, "Think for Yourself", we looked at the unique nature of individual thought, and recognised the tendency for people to look at things from their own point of view in preference to other opinions. The aim then, was to encourage *you* to think things out for *yourself* without being unduly influenced by other people. The intention now, is to look more closely at the way *other people* think. This will help you to recognise, and maybe resolve, differences of opinion, and will enable you to present your own case with maximum benefit. It will also help you to handle relationships, and lead you to a better understanding of yourself.

To begin, we must ask the question "What makes people think differently?". In broad terms, the answer is differences of knowledge and experience, but there are three main qualifications which also need to be studied. These are:-

1. Status, position and group allegiance;
2. Substance; and
3. Emotion.

Each of these will be considered in turn, in the next three chapters, and on completion you will have a full picture of the causes of differences between people. We must begin, however, with knowledge and experience.

KNOWLEDGE AND EXPERIENCE.

In Part I of this book, I referred to the framework, or structure, within which most of our thinking takes place. I mentioned, on the one hand, the concrete facts and universally held rules and, on the other, the abstract ideas and personal experiences. These are illustrated in this diagram:-

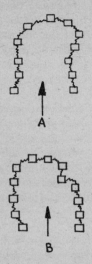

The diagram represents the thinking structures of two individuals, A and B. The blocks are the concrete facts which are common to both structures. The squiggles are the abstract ideas and experiences which differ between the individuals. This causes the overall shape of the structures to be different, which leads to them thinking differently on some subjects.

In the main, differences of opinion between individuals remain at a non-consequential level. However, there is always a possibility that differences will lead to open disagreement. When this happens, it is often advisable to identify the point of difference, so that some attempt can be made to resolve it. In order to do this, there are four main checks which can be made:

Check 1: Agreement on subject of problem.
Make sure that each of the parties in dispute is referring to the same subject.

 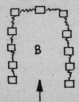

This means checking communication and interpretation.

a) Communication: Many differences arise simply because of misunderstanding due to poor communication. Each person knows what he, himself, thinks, but it is not always easy to put ideas into words for communication to another person. Apart from this, errors can arise when transmitting or receiving information. How often have you heard accomplished public speakers unwittingly use what is obviously an incorrect word? In addition to this it is very easy to mishear hurried, or muffled speech. Mistakes occur in written words too.

Errors can also be caused by non-communication, such as when one person changes the subject without informing the other. When two people are engaged in conversation, it is common for them to switch alternately from one subject to another, each person concentrating on his own interest, and only listening vaguely to the other. This increases the likelihood of a misunderstanding, and is frequently used as a source of comedy in T.V. and theatre farces.

b) Interpretation: Differences of interpretation can also cause conflict. This is particularly so when an expert is communicating with a layman on a specialised subject. Extra care should be taken by both sides in these cases. Similar confusion can arise due to local, or national, variations in the use of a word or phrase, or some other ambiguity.

Non-verbal communication may also be misinterpreted. Attitude, posture, tone of voice, etc. all serve to create an emotional background to any exchange between individuals. People are not always aware of this form of communication, but its importance can perhaps be judged from the degree of attention given to it by sales staff, and others who use it as a means of persuasion to win custom. From your own point of view, don't be unduly influenced by non-verbal signals from other people, and try not to transmit unhelpful signals yourself. I will say more about emotions, later.

In order to eliminate problems of communication and interpretation, it is useful at an early stage, for each person to state his understanding of what the other said. This provides an opportunity for corrections to be made if necessary.

Check 2. Agreement on concrete facts.
The second check is to ensure agreement on the main facts. It may be that your case is greatly influenced by a piece of information which is unknown to the other person. To overcome this difficulty it is often useful to list the main facts to the other person. It is also possible that your opponent is basing his case on incorrect information, which you should attempt to identify and put right. It could be, of course, that the mistake is yours, in which case you can resolve the conflict very quickly, if you choose.

This diagram indicates the checking of main facts to identify differences.

Check 3. Agreement on validity of previous experience.
The cause of dispute may be a wide difference of personal experience. Each of you will assume, consciously or sub-consciously, that your personal experience is typical, and can be relied on to judge new situations. There will be total impasse if you each assume that your limited experience gives you absolute knowledge of the subject. You may each have a possible interpretation, but your conflicting interpretations cannot both be probable.

This diagram illustrates the checking of individual experiences.

You may be able to agree on the relative merits of each other's experiences, or you may seek further evidence, by testing or asking other people. It is likely that the best interpretation will lie somewhere between the two extremes, so that you may both have to make some concessions if agreement is to be reached.

Check 4. Agreement on mental process.

There may still be a difference of opinion despite there being no errors of communication, and both parties being aware of all the facts. In these cases, the difference could arise from differences in logical construction.

The diagram
illustrates the need
for checking the
process of arriving
at the answer.

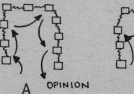

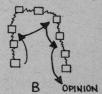

A OPINION   B OPINION

It should help if you each examine the other's chain of thought, as this may provide a fresh way of looking at the problem. In your case, try to present the information in a way which appeals to the other person, and gives you a favourable outcome.

If you have satisfied these four checks and are still not able to reach agreement, then you should consider whether differences of status and position are the root cause of the disagreement.

20
THAT'S WHAT YOU THINK
STATUS, POSITION, AND GROUP ALLEGIANCE

Individuals are strongly influenced in their thinking by the effect which the outcome will have on their current position. The reason is, either the need to protect that position, or to fulfil the expectations of their particular role. For example, a student and his teacher will think differently. The student may think, "I must pass this exam in order to get a job", whereas the teacher may think, "He must pass this exam so that I can demonstrate that I am a successful teacher".

In this example, there is unlikely to be any major conflict because, although the teacher and student have different motives, they have a common interest in the student passing the exam. There are many cases, however, where there is a difference of both motive and interest, and these are a source of potential conflict. In a work situation, for example, the employer is interested in making a profit, and sees his workers as a means of producing that end. They are one of the factors of production to be managed. From the employee's point of view, the job gives him a living, and he is not usually going to extend himself merely to make extra profits unless there is some benefit in it for him. In the main, the employer/employee relationship survives on the basis of mutual benefit, but conflicts of interest do arise from time to time to test the industrial relations skills of management and the unions.

Differences of opinion flowing from differences of position can be explained in diagramatic terms by introducing a third dimension to the structure previously considered. We have hitherto thought of the structure in two dimensions only as illustrated overleaf:-

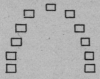

It is difficult to illustrate the third dimension on paper but a visible picture may be imagined when likened to a side of bacon on a butcher's slicing machine. The end-on view of the bacon changes slightly as each new slice is cut. The thicker the slice, the more noticeable will be the difference of the end-on view. Likewise, the wider the difference of position between two individuals, the more noticeable will be their difference of opinion. We can now see how people with apparently similar structures can have different points of view on a particular subject.

A more useful analogy for this third dimension, however, is that of a telescope or other optical instrument such as a camera. The overall view through the lens may be kept constant while the focal length is altered from close-up to infinity. The effect will be to change the subject in focus, blurring everything else. If it is assumed that a person's position determines the focal length of his view of a problem, then it follows that differences of position will result in differences of opinion. The wider the difference of position, the more blurred will be an individual's view of his opponent's stance.

It is often useful to consider the other person's position in relation to the subject under consideration. I am not suggesting that you should be suspicious of his motives, or untrusting, but it will help you to realise that other people do not always see things the way you do. Ask yourself the question, "What's in it for him?", or, "What's he looking for?". This will enable you to shape the way you present your case to him. You can concentrate on those areas which are most likely to influence him, and save energy on the areas which, to him, are of little consequence.

For example, suppose, as a business manager, you want planning permission to extend your transport depot onto adjoining farm land. There is no point telling the planning officer that it is to help you rationalise your business to achieve economies. He will be more interested if you explain that the extension will enable you to improve the use and overall appearance of the depot, and park your drivers' cars off the residential streets, to the benefit of the neighbourhood. The details of your proposed economies will be of more interest to the bank, should you wish to seek an advance to finance the works.

It is not always sufficient merely to look at the subject from the other person's point of view. You should try to imagine that you *are* that other person. This method has often been used by the military, or police, in attempting to predict the movements of the opposition, or a fugitive. It can be used equally effectively in business. The point is, that you may see the same things differently, through the eyes of that other person. Remember, he is in a different position, so he thinks differently.

FIXED AND VARIABLE POSITIONS

Identifying the other person's position is not always easy and is made more difficult by the fact that it may change from time to time. Such changes may be progressive, alternate, or parallel, and may on occasions be deliberately hidden. Each of these changes will be considered separately.

1. *Progressive changes.*

These are easiest to identify because they are most definite. Examples of progressive change include a child growing up to become a parent, and an office junior becoming a senior manager. You will probably have recognised a change in attitude of someone you know who has made a progressive step.

2. *Alternate changes.*

These are somewhat perplexing and yet very revealing of human nature. A classic example is the motorist/pedestrian. A motorist may blast his horn at a pedestrian who gets in his way, and later, as a pedestrian himself, will curse another motorist who does the same to him. The alternate change may be less evident than the example just given. In one of the parables of Jesus, a servant owed the King a substantial sum of money which he could not repay. The king ordered him to be sold as a slave together with his wife and children. The servant pleaded for mercy, and the king forgave him the debt and let him go. Shortly after, the man met one of his fellow servants who owed him a small sum. He grabbed him by the throat and demanded instant repayment. The fellow servant begged for mercy, but was refused, and thrown into jail.

3.   Parallel interests.

An example of this would arise if an M.P. found that his holiday cottage was affected by a government proposal for a new airport. Having parallel interests is often referred to as wearing two or more hats. The individual may make his position clear by stating which hat he is wearing at the particular moment, or you may have to ask him directly. In the case of formal meetings, if the parallel interest is likely to influence an individual's view, it is normal for him to declare the interest, and withdraw from the discussion and vote. The purpose of mentioning parallel interests here is so that you can be aware of the need to check which position is having greatest influence on the person with whom you are in dispute.

4.   Hidden agenda.

Sometimes, you may not be aware of the parallel interest, and the other party may choose not to disclose it. In these cases the undisclosed interest may be referred to as "hidden agenda". (Incidently, hidden agenda includes any secret parallel motive, whether or not it arises from a secret position). There is no guaranteed method for exposing hidden agenda, and it will often remain harmless and undetected. In the context of this chapter, however, the problem arises when it obstructs the settlement of a parallel open dispute.

For example, let us assume, with a little stretch of imagination, that the M.P. in the earlier example is appointed chairman of the committee searching for a new airport. Assume also that he keeps quiet about the location of his holiday cottage. The experts on the committee may have strong reasons for the selection of the site which happens to be close to the M.P's home. In order to defend his hidden position, the M.P. will have to oppose the expert advice, and perhaps offer a suggestion for a better airport location. In this situation, the experts would find it very difficult to reason with the M.P.

Although the precise nature of hidden agenda is difficult to detect, it may at least be possible to identify its existence. The reason for this is that hidden agenda is difficult to sustain in any debate. The visible argument, behind which the undisclosed interest is hidden, becomes progressively more difficult to uphold, because it has no main substance. In this respect, it is very like the magician's trick, described earlier. The magician is able to maintain secrecy only because he dictates what his audience is allowed to see. Few tricks could survive uncontrolled scrutiny by the audience. Likewise, hidden agenda does not stand up well to close examination. Hidden agenda may be suspected if someone becomes very irrational in debate, or switches frantically from one lost cause to another without admitting defeat.

REACHING AGREEMENT
The purpose of looking at the other person's point of view is, where possible, to reach agreement on beneficial terms. In the case of disagreements arising from differences of knowledge and experience, the aim should be to share information by examination and cross-examination, until consensus is reached.

Conflicts arising from differences of position are unlikely to be resolved by consensus because one or other of the persons in dispute would have to give up his position. Differences of this nature are more often settled by compromise. This means that you may have to settle for something less than your ideal, in a trade-off negotiation. The sacrifice need not be too great, however, because each of you is likely to have different priorities. Here again, it is useful to consider the other person's viewpoint so that you can identify the areas which are likely to be important to him, but are of little consequence to you, and vice versa.

EFFECTS OF GROUPS ON THINKING POSITION
In this chapter so far, we have been looking at the differences of opinion which arise in a closed encounter with another person. We now need to widen this to consider how an individual's thinking may be influenced by the many different people with whom he comes into contact, and the wide range of subjects

likely to be covered.

It is sometimes said that two people are "poles apart" in their individual views of a particular subject, and I want to use this analogy to illustrate how these differences can arise. I will use the north/south axis to explain changes of elevation, and the east/west axis for changes of association.

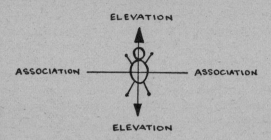

Changes of elevation

Human beings have an inherent desire, both to be individual, and to belong to a group. This apparent contradiction is explained by the need, on one hand, for self expression, and on the other, for protection and survival. The effect of this is to produce a variety of responses from an individual depending on the people with whom he is currently in contact. To illustrate this I will use the subject of supporting a football team. You will probably have your own favourite team and will be prepared to defend it in any discussion with a rival supporter. Follow through the stages listed below, and notice how the argument changes. You will also see at which point you could agree with these statements which might be made by a Liverpool supporter.

1.   I support Liverpool F.C. because they are best.

2.   Liverpool are better than Everton.

3.   Liverpool and Everton are better than Manchester United and Manchester City.

4.   Liverpool, Everton, Man. Utd., and Man City, are better than the Midlands clubs such as Aston Villa and Forest.

5.   The northern clubs, eg. Liverpool, Man. Utd., Forest and Everton, are better than Arsenal, Spurs, West Ham and the other London clubs.

6.   English clubs are better than Scottish clubs.

7.   British clubs are better than European clubs.

8.   And so on.

It will be seen that the argument for, or against, Manchester United, depends on whom the Liverpool supporter is talking to. The tendency will be to retreat to the defence of the group immediately below the level of current contention. (In reality today, geographical loyalty is not as strong as I have indicated here, but the principle still remains valid). This process also operates in reverse, for in a debate with fellow Liverpool supporters, it is likely that they would not agree on the relative merits of individual players.

The same principle applies to many other subjects such as religion, nationality, politics. The level of the individual's thinking will be determined by external circumstances, and will be elevated to a new position should circumstances change. For example, there will be differences of opinion within a trade union which may be the subject of heated debate at branch meetings. In any dispute with another union, however, it is likely that the members will shelve their differences, and present themselves as a single unit. Likewise, as members of the T.U.C., the member unions will overlook their differences in any discussions with government. The lower level of conflict will, of course, resurface when the influence of external circumstances diminishes.

This was the principle underlying Caesar's policy of "divide and rule". People will shelve their differences and unite to fight a common cause. In order to reduce the strength of a combined attack, it will be advantageous to highlight the underlying differences between the members of the combined force.

Changes of association. (The east–west axis)

Individuals belong to many formal, and informal, groups which match, and even influence their thinking. Consider, for example, the following distinctive groups, and note those to which you belong:-

1. Sex – Male/Female.
2. Age group – Teenage, young adult, middle age, old age.
3. Motorist/Non-motorist.
4. C.N.D. supporter/Supporter of a nuclear deterrent.
5. Smoker/Non-smoker.
6. Dog owner/no dog.
7. Sports club member – Squash, tennis, golf, judo, rugby, etc.
8. Churchgoer/Non-churchgoer.
9. Righthanded/Lefthanded.
10. Parent/no children.

Even with this small sample of subjects, it is unlikely that you will find many people who match your groupings precisely. In any contact with another person, you will find some subjects in which you have a common interest, and others where you will differ. In general, the differences will be of no consequence and your relationship will remain harmonious. They are a potential source of conflict, however, which may surface at any time, either by choice, or due to some external influence. When this happens, you may each be forced to defend your own particular group against the other. It is at this stage that an understanding of the other person's view will be useful, as this will enable you to gauge the likelihood of reaching agreement. Often, when differences of this nature arise, each person has a deep rooted loyalty to his particular group and will not be persuaded to change his mind. Continued debate may, therefore, be fruitless, and may only widen the difference.

Even though groups are not always visibly identifiable, they are constantly forming and reforming. In this respect they may be likened to a kaleidoscope where the various pieces may be moved over and over again, yet always remain in a pattern. If you take a random collection of people, you will find that their alliances change, as the focal subject of conversation changes. If, in these circumstances, you find yourself in a minority, and decide that it is unlikely that you will convert the opposition to your view, you may wish to change the subject to one which will put you in a majority position.

This principle of alliance applies at all levels. For example, consider the international boycotting of major sporting events such as the Olympic Games. One of the major countries identifies an apparent misdemeanour of another, which is never very hard, and uses it as a reason to pull out of the games. It is very unlikely that such action will produce an apology from the "offender". Instead, the supporters of each of the disputing nations rally together in their opposing groups, with one group feeling obliged to join the boycott. Countries from either side may attempt to switch the focal subject back to sport, and one or two may waver, but the complainant country will persist with its original objection. This is a very comfortable game of international politics. It is a game, because the focal subject for dispute is chosen at random from a large selection of issues. It is comfortable, because normal trading, military and political positions remain unaffected, while the only risk is the sacrifice required of the sportsmen. It would be interesting to see what would happen if the sportsmen and women of the world decided to choose sport as their focal subject, and ignored the petty whims of their respective politicians. The sportsmen would benefit, but the politicians would lose their soft weapon. Maybe for this reason, it wouldn't be such a good idea after all.

CONCLUSION
In your contacts with other people, you should now be able to identify causes of dispute, and appreciate the effect of differences of position. This should enable you to resolve, or avoid conflict, and seek opportunities for mutual benefit, but there may still be some difficulty, and the next chapter contains some further checks which can be made.

21
THAT'S WHAT YOU THINK (III)
SUBSTANCE: A.B.C. THINKING

It is well known that the brain is comprised of two halves. The right side of the brain handles abstract ideas, perceptions, feelings and artistic appreciation; while the left side deals in logic, facts and concrete ideas. Everybody uses both halves, although not necessarily with the same bias or degree of consistency. Each of us has a leaning in a particular direction, in the same way that one might have a leaning towards right or left in politics. And as in politics, this may vary from time to time, or even subject to subject. Most people will be somewhere in the middle, where they make a balanced use of the two sides of their brain. Some people, however, demonstrate in their behaviour, a strong leaning towards one side or the other.

The two extremes are, on the one side ABSTRACT (A), and on the other, CONCRETE (C). In the middle is the BALANCED (B) position. Hence my use of the description "A B C Thinking". It will be useful to imagine this as a balancing scale, thus:-

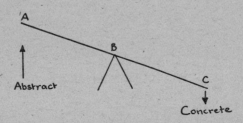

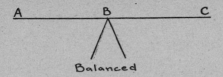

Balanced

Although a great deal of thinking takes place around the balanced position, we shall see that it is possible to influence this position consciously. In order to assist this, it will be helpful, for the time being, to consider the extremes in absolute terms.

Referring back to the diagram used earlier in this book, the abstract thinker places a greater emphasis on the abstract squiggles, whereas the concrete thinker relies more on the concrete boxes.

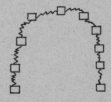

It can be seen from this that two people with similar structures might have a disagreement if one is concrete, and the other, abstract. Consider the following story:-

Mr. C. has fallen through a hole in the middle of an ice covered pond, having obviously miscalculated the distribution of his weight in relation to its load-bearing capacity. His lady friend, Miss A. had a feeling that this was going to happen, and had warned him, but to no avail. Mr. C. appealed to her for help, but although she could see his problem, she could not think of an immediate solution. Mr. C. noticed a rope hanging from a nearby tree, and told Miss A. to untie it and use it to pull him out. Miss A. was reluctant to do this, fearing that she would be pulled into the hole with him. She ignored his suggestion about the rope, and explained that she would go and look for a ladder. Mr. C. could not see a ladder, and demanded that she threw him the rope. She refused to discuss anything other than the ladder and so they just carried on shouting at each other. The more they shouted, the less likely it was that they would reach agreement.

Many disagreements in everyday life are like that, although not always so clearly so. There is no dispute about the problem, or its need for a solution, but the abstract and concrete agruments are not on the same plane and will not find common ground. In the story, the concrete man wanted to deal logically with the facts as he could see them, and was not interested in woolly abstract ideas he could not see. (His thinking may also have been influenced by his POSITION in the pond as previously discussed, or by his EMOTION, to be discussed next). The abstract girl, did not want to use the rope, nor did she want to be drawn into a detailed argument about her reasons, fearing she may lose the argument, and be pulled into the pond. She was safest, sticking to her abstract idea about the ladder.

It is easy to see how situations like this can arise, and you may already know one or two people who would be likely to adopt one of these two stances. Certainly, some people do display clear characteristics of being concrete or abstract. There is also a tendency for people in particular jobs to have a leaning in one direction. Architects, for example, are likely to be abstract, while engineers tend to be concrete.

I am not suggesting that either side is superior or preferable to the other, merely that they are different; and somewhere in the middle is the balanced view. Now this balanced position is interesting because it suggests that one may incorporate the qualities of both extremes. Indeed, do not forget that our brains comprise both halves, so this must be possible in practice.

What then, determines which side will predominate, and can this domination be reversed? Even if it can, is there any benefit to be obtained? In my view, the answer is that it is partly inherent, and partly due to the external environment. Some change of emphasis can be achieved by conscious effort, and as I will demonstrate, substantial rewards can result.

Let us look first at the evidence. Some people appear to be exclusively abstract or concrete in every sphere of their lives, while others vary in different spheres. For example, a bank manager may be very concrete in his work, but abstract in his role on a local committee. Other people may vary between abstract and concrete in a single role, and this is very interesting. Mrs. Thatcher, for example, in her role as Prime Minister, has been admired internationally for her analytical mind, and her ability to argue her case in logical, concrete terms. On the other hand, she was able to make abstract decisions, (e.g. introduction of poll tax) without perhaps having first stated publicly the logical, supporting argument. Much of this was left to her Ministers, fellow M.P.s and civil servants.

The evidence suggests that we do have some choice in the matter. The next question is, which to choose? To answer this we must look at the advantages and disadvantages of the two distinct styles.

CONCRETE

The concrete person tends to be an expert in his own field, or is aiming to be. He has accumulated a lot of experience and is familiar with his environment. He may, however, be reluctant to expand, or change, his environment unless he is absolutely sure that the new ground is better. In general, he will be task oriented, believing that his work will speak for him, and will work well in a team, provided that too is task oriented. Any research and development will be by logical progression, and he will be reluctant to take chances. Indeed, absence of logic will tend to cause mental agoraphobia.

At his worst, he is a worrier, often being premature in identifying problems. He may have some difficulty progressing into higher management if:-

a) it removes him from close contact with his familiar environment and he is not directly involved in producing his normal work; or

b) it involves him in having to take decisions without the comfort and security of a fully worked up and proven plan.

In terms of his own self development, he will lack the confidence to strike for the top until he is satisfied that he is 100% ready and deserving. As this is unlikely to happen very often, few concrete men make it to the top.

Advantages, Disadvantages and Choice.
As you can see, the main advantage of concrete thinking is the attention to detail, and reliability of logic. The disadvantage is

the reluctance to take risks outside the logical framework. The choice is to make a positive effort to relax the thinking structure, and allow scope for more intuition.

Advice to the concrete thinker:
Continue to develop ideas logically but be prepared to take a few risks, and in this context many of the earlier mentioned techniques for breaking out of structured thinking will be very useful. Try to exercise conscious control. Think about self projection and image. Make sure that you get the credit for a job well done, and make people more aware of your presence. Stop using your own imperfections as a reason for holding back. Take a risk. That is what abstract people do. Concrete thinking may be appropriate in many circumstances, but do not dismiss the benefits which abstract thinking can produce.

ABSTRACT

The abstract person's particular strength is his intuition and feeling. In sport, music and the arts, it expresses itself in the spontaneity which produces "purple patch" performances. It can all be lost if too much attention is paid to detail. For this reason, the abstract person prefers to be more of a generalist and avoids getting bogged down in detail. Logic can be very claustrophobic. In business and contact with others, he leaves details to the experts (although he would not necessarily accept that he was not himself an expert). He is not very familiar with the "nuts and bolts" of the job, but knows whom he can rely on for advice and support. He is, therefore, more of a planner and organiser than a producer, and may describe himself as a man manager. He will tend to concentrate his efforts on the high profile elements of his job, presentation and image being very important, both in terms of personal projection and job output. The work will not speak for itself.

He will be fairly receptive to change, not being attached to any particular environment, and may, in fact, be the instigator of change within his organisation. "How do we know it's not better if we don't try it?"

He is particularly good at decision making for a number of reasons:-

a)   His broad view often obscures difficulties.
b)   He is able to see beyond difficulties by suspending logic and focusing on the objective.
c)   He often relies on the efforts of other people to fulfil the decision.
d)   He allocates additional resources, or switches resources to overcome difficulties.
e)   If all else fails, he moves the goalposts, or even himself, to pastures new.

In terms of self development and projection, he will be more confident to strike for the top having regard to his self image and his man management and decision making skills.

Advantages, Disadvantages and Choice
The main advantage of abstract thinking is the use of that part of the brain which is not accessible consciously. It therefore provides an extension to normal thinking capacity. In addition, it encourages a broad view which can more easily break through structured thinking. The disadvantage is the reluctance to become involved in detail, for fear of being encapsulated by logic.

Advice to the abstract thinker:
The choice is to develop some concrete ideas in the field of your own choosing. Select a particular subject, maybe a developing sector within your job, and preferably high profile, and make yourself an expert in this field. This will earn you greater respect from your concrete colleagues, and you will be the envy of your colleagues with abstract leanings. More importantly, you will have introduced balance to your style.

A.B.C. THINKING. VARIATION OF APPROACH
There is another area in which you may choose which approach to adopt. Up to now, I have referred to the abstract and concrete extremes in absolute terms, when more realistically they are leanings either side of centre. Furthermore, they are personal to each individual, and relative. To explain this, let me use again the analogy of political leanings to right and left. The spectrum is so broad, that no matter where you consider yourself to be,

there will be some people to the right of you, and others to the left. Similarly with the A-B-C spectrum, you will meet people who are more concrete than you, and some who are more abstract.

In general, the person who knows more about a particular subject than you, is likely to be more concrete. This is because his superior knowledge would give him the advantage in any detailed discussion. If he chose to, he could "blind you with science". Somebody who is less knowledgeable than you on any given subject, is likely to be more abstract, and will prefer to discuss the matter "in broad terms", which puts you in the concrete position, if you choose to take it.

You will see from this, that the position may change according to the subject under discussion, and the parties to that discussion. Also there is an opportunity for choice.

At this stage, I should say that my definition of the word "abstract" is itself somewhat abstract. It is intended to describe not only woolly thinkers who operate by using bluff and avoidance tactics, but also those who choose to be remote or intangible, and prefer to take a broad view.

Now consider some examples of this choice.

1.　*The Falklands incident.* At the beginning of the conflict, the Argentinians took concrete action by occupying the islands. In the discussions which followed, however, they adopted abstract tactics, by being visibly prepared to TALK about the problem, but unwilling to withdraw or declare open war. The British response was to seek a concrete conclusion to the talks followed by the concrete action of retaking the islands by force.

2.　*Political campaigns.* Very often political campaigns avoid addressing the main issues. Policies are discussed in broad terms only. This abstract, umbrella approach appeals to a much broader spectrum of voters than would a set of detailed policies presented in detailed, concrete terms. The more concrete the policy, the more opportunity there is for disagreement. This is because everybody is different, and ultimate focusing on a subject will maximise the differences of opinion between individuals.

3.　*Project management.* A project manager usually leads a

multi-professional team. He does not need to know the concrete details of each professional's specialism, but can deal with them in abstract terms, relying on their individual skills to produce the required output. This abstract view will enable the manager to push the job along, and detect any problems which may call for more concrete attention.

4. *Salesmanship*. Salespersons should have a good knowledge of the products they wish to sell, and should be able to relate the benefits to the potential customers. As each customer is different, so the salesperson must be able to vary the approach to maximise the appeal. In this context it may be prefereable to begin the sales presentation in abstract terms, because this will have broadest appeal, and switch to concrete detail as required by the customer. Clearly each case has to be treated on its own merits, but will be useful to the salesperson to be aware of the two possible approaches, so that the right one can be adopted at the appropriate time.

BUSINESS MANAGEMENT
Any business organisation is likely to have a mix of A and C personnel. The question for management is whether this mix is right, or whether reallocation or training is required. Also the A.B.C. profile needs to be checked at the time of staff selection in order to maintain a good balance. This subject is quite complex, and beyond the scope of this book, which is essentially concerned with the differences in the way we each think. Nevertheless, some consideration of organisations will be helpful in the present context.

Head of Organisation: It is a matter of some contention whether the head of an organisation should be a concrete person with the same professional background and expert knowledge as the staff; or whether this should be an abstract person from a different background. For reasons given, some abstract qualities will be required, and as such an abstract person will be preferred, although the ideal could be a concrete person with abstract balance.

Senior staff: Here there should be a mix of concrete and abstract people, although again, balance is preferable. There are often too many abstract people at this level. Health authorities, for example, are thought by many to have an excess of administrators, and insufficient focus on provision of services to patients. I have also heard views expressed in two universities that one of the problems of the British engineering industry is that concrete personnel rarely progress into senior management positions, these being held almost entirely by abstract people. Apparently the same is not true in U.S.A. and Japan.

CONCLUSION
Recognising these differences of substance should prove helpful in identifying the source of some differences of opinion, which in turn should assist the settlement of those differences.

QUOTE: *The trouble with the World is that the ignorant are cocksure and the intelligent are full of self-doubt.*

22
THAT'S WHAT YOU THINK (IV)
EMOTIONS

The aim of this chapter is to examine emotions and their effect on our thinking, particularly those which lead to differences of opinion.

As I have already said, the purpose of our brain is to aid our survival and development. Because it operates on the basis of accumulated knowledge and experience, our individual thinking is very self-centred, or subjective. Our view of the world is, therefore, very egocentric, and it is in this context that emotions are most relevant. In order to consider these, it will be useful to have a diagrammatic model.

First, imagine yourself at the centre of a number of concentric circles, as illustrated:

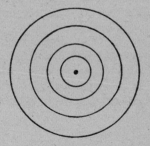

Let us consider first, the emotion of LOVE.

Now let us assume for a moment that you have broken your arm. That would be pretty important to you wouldn't it? Picture yourself on the centre spot, perhaps feeling a little sorry for yourself. After all, your arm hurts and the nature of your injury has inconvenienced your normal routine. It is certainly not something which can be ignored in your everyday thinking.

Now, forget about your arm being broken, and think of those people in your life who, if they broke their arm, you might perhaps prefer that it was your own arm that had been broken. There will not be many in this category, which will be limited to very close family and friends. Imagine these people in the innermost circle of your diagram, as the people who mean most to you. In the next circle from the centre will be those people in your life who, if they broke their arm, would receive your full sympathy and attention, but not to the extent that you would prefer to suffer the injury yourself. And in the next circle would be those to whom you would express some comment of consolation, while in the next would be those to whom you would not feel it necessary to say anything. And so on.

The inner circle contains not only the people, but also the things which mean most to you. It is your home base to where you may retreat, and from where you project your feelings. Love is a positive emotion, and in diagramatic terms, the rings spread out to encompass love objects. These are then contained within the inner circles. The more loving the individual, the wider will be these rings. People with a wide circle of friends enjoy the comfort and pleasure of this. There is a limit, however, to the effective capacity of the innermost circles. For example, nurses and others involved in the caring services cannot perform effectively if they become too emotionally involved with those in their care.

These rings are not just designed to contain the things we love – they also act as defences to keep out the things we do not like. If any thing or person threatens us, then we can retreat towards to centre behind the rings. The question of which ring depends on the relative strength of the threat. The aim is to shut it out as

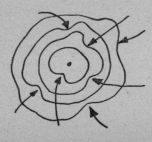

Attacks on
the Egocentre

far away from the centre as possible in order to maximise the "defended space". See diagram.

War is unpleasant – we shut it out. How close are we to it? Even those directly involved, civilians or military, have to survive mentally, and to do so they have to use this process; although clearly, the defensive ring will be very close to the centre. Others see warfare on T.V. and can become immune to it. This applies not just to war of course, but also redundancy, famine, disaster, car accidents, aeroplane crashes, etc. In the main they are kept at a distance, but occasionally they penetrate the outer rings.

If you actually witness a car accident, for example, you are likely to drive more carefully, for a time at least – until the penetrated rings repair themselves. Time is said to be the great healer. Every motorist must be aware of the dangers of driving at high speeds. There is enough evidence of this, and yet many persist in doing it. That is the effect of these defensive rings. Where logic may call for caution, these rings enable motorists to imagine that accidents only happen to other people.

Press coverage of disasters is interesting. Some papers report unemotional facts, while others deliberately look for, and project, a human angle in an attempt to penetrate the outer rings and appeal to their readers' emotions. These are the same barriers that advertisers and salesmen have to break through to achieve their aims.

It can be seen then that the function of these rings is to control the protection and expansion of the egocentre, and all our emotions can be viewed in these terms. For example:-

Hate: is directed at anything or anyone who appears to be threatening the centre. The closer to the centre, the more powerful the feeling.

Envy: is directed at another egocentre which appears to be performing better than the subject egocentre, thereby making it feel inferior and threatened.

Pride: is the expansive projection of the subject egocentre against any apparent challengers.

Joy: is a feeling of wellbeing within the egocentre.

Lust: is a desire to draw into the centre, something which will aid the comfort of, or enhance reputation of, the egocentre.

WHY DO WE HAVE EMOTIONS? WHAT HAPPENS TO OUR THINKING?

Remember, the aim of the brain is to assist our survival and development, and it achieves this to a large extent by logical processing and retention of information in its memory bank. There will be occasions, however, when normal logic will not produce enough urgency or energy to satisfy this aim. Emotions close options and create blinkers, so that thinking energy is concentrated on a small area, in the same way as a laser beam focuses energy on a target. This can be illustrated in terms of our diagram:-

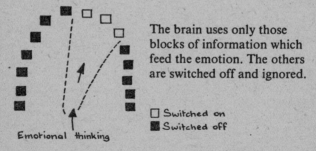

The brain uses only those blocks of information which feed the emotion. The others are switched off and ignored.

☐ Switched on
■ Switched off

Emotional thinking

Falling in love is emotional, and lovers are often described as being "blind" to logic. War too, is often illogical. Viewed from a distance, most disputes seem trivial. The people involved are emotionally blinded, and are receptive only to propaganda which fuels that emotion.

Sometimes emotional focusing can be counter productive. The more immediate the threat, the stronger the emotion; and the stronger the emotion, the more blinkered the thinking. For example, people calling emergency services often forget to give sufficient information as to the address of the incident. The telephone conversation often goes like this. "Come quickly, there's a fire." "Where is it?" "In the kitchen. Hurry.", and the caller hangs up. What is frightening is that the emotional thinker is oblivious of the error. I will return to this, later.

EMOTION WINDOW
Emotions are largely a product of the subconscious, and therefore not easily controlled. They are triggered when the brain decides that special attention needs to be focused on a particular issue for the protection or development of the egocentre. In order to monitor this, all incoming information passes through an emotion window in the brain for vetting. If anything represents a threat or potential benefit to the egocentre then it is flagged and brought to attention. If it is serious, then other information sources will be cut off to ensure maximum attention is given to the particular issue. If it is of only minor importance, then attention will still be drawn to it, but there will be a minimal information cut off, and logical thought will probably suppress the emotion. This may not be enough to obliterate the issue, which may surface again a few times before it is finally dealt with.

CONTACT WITH OTHERS
Any contact with other people may produce an emotional response. Whether by verbal, or non-verbal communication, your approach may be regarded as welcome or threatening. To be welcomed, your approach must be seen to be beneficial to the other party. If the contact is for business purposes, say to offer a product for sale, then the emphasis should be placed on the benefits to be obtained rather than the objective qualities, or features of the product. If, on the other hand, the sales person alienates the potential customer, the barriers will come up and no amount of logical explanation will persuade him to accept the proposal.

GENERAL OBSERVATIONS
Before concluding this chapter let us consider a number of business and personal circumstances which involve emotional thinking. This will assist understanding of emotions generally, and provide a guide in dealing with similar specific cases.

1. *Security Zones and Stress Thresholds*
Security zones are represented by the inner circles of our diagrammatic egocentre. This home base is a vital refuge in the individual's contact with the world. The more secure this base,

the more able the individual is to cope with the outside hostilities and difficulties. See diagram:

The stress threshold is the extent to which the egocentre can withstand attacks on its centre. Any event which potentially diminishes the security of the centre zone will have an emotional impact on the egocentre, e.g. change of job, change of house, bereavement or other loss. These events will draw on the reserves of the egocentre, and only time, support and diversionary activities will redress the damage. Too many attacks of this nature at any one time may cause serious, long-term damage, and attempts should therefore be made to avoid generating new problems if the egocentre is already under severe attack. See diagram:

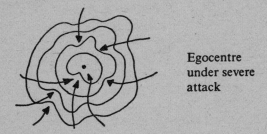

Egocentre under severe attack

2.   Crisis Management

Emotional thinking may affect not only individuals, but also partnerships, and larger corporate groups including businesses. The business becomes the egocentre with the joint aims of survival and development. If a crisis threatens the business then the emotional response is to focus energy on that crisis, and this will often produce high adrenalin performances from the staff. This is good, but as with individual emotional thinking, some blinkering may have crept in, and care should be taken to ensure that an oversight does not produce other problems. Also, for this reason, the introduction of artificial crises to motivate staff may be counter productive.

3.   Workaholics

Some people become irrationally hooked on their work. This is an emotional reaction which can be caused by any of the following reasons among others:-

a)   The individual identifies personally with the business egocentre. Any attack on the business, or any opportunity for business expansion is viewed with personal emotion, and the blinkering effect of the emotion obscures everything outside that narrow scope.

b)   The individual is very ambitious and is driven on by this emotion.

c)   The individual is attempting to secure a sound base by expending excess energy now, in order to create space for relaxation later. He sees himself in a dark tunnel and hopes that the light at the end will soon get larger. It rarely does, but his emotion will not let him see that.

4.   Rewards and Recognition

The aim of each individual is survival and development, and his efforts are employed to this end. In diagrammatic terms this is achieved by enlarging and enhancing the central security zone, and pushing out some of the boundaries of the outer rings. This is where people differ. Some are power conscious, and want to develop the outer rings to their maximum extent, while others are content with a smaller sphere of comfort. In either event, some effort is required to achieve these desires. The reward for this effort may be in cash or kind, and both are necessary. Because we are dealing with emotion however, these in themselves will not be sufficient. They have to be converted into comforts within the egocentre. There are of course other ways of comforting the egocentre, one of which is recognition. For this reason, recognition for achievement is very important, and in the business world its value as a management tool should not be underestimated.

5. *Macho Motoring*

The desire to develop and expand is both individual and collective, and is the driving force which motivates mankind. It was this that led man to step on the moon, and the emotion of that success was felt by the whole world, because it uplifted each one of us and expanded the frontiers of human achievement. At a personal level, the symbol of this desire is speed, power and size, hence the fascination with anything human or mechanical which can deliver these. This desire is only really satisfied, however, by participation, and the easiest outlet for this is the motor car. It might be thrilling to travel on Concorde at Mach 2, but that does not satisfy the Mach 0 because it is not personal enough. The motor car is personal, and may be regarded as an extension of the personality of the driver. The driver and the car become one. Its power and speed potential become his, and unless he is able to control these feelings, the likelihood is he will want to demonstrate them to his fellow motorists, and will take offence if another motorist dares to trespass on his territory by overtaking or cutting in.

6. *Love, Marriage and Domestic Strife*

I have already described the emotion of Love which involves a reaching out of the egocentric rings to encompass, and draw in, the love object. In any romance, this is a two way process. Each of the partners draws the other into their egocentre. As the relationship develops, and the interests of the two merge, so there develops a partnership egocentre. This has the same characteristics as the personal egocentre, but two nuclei. See diagram:

What is important to the well-being of this double-nucleus egocentre, is that the partners must work together for its protection, expansion, and enhancement of the inner area. This is not easy because it involves two separate individuals who, no matter how close, each have their own ideas and aspirations which will occasionally conflict. Also, they must relate to the outside world as well as to themselves, and it must be remembered that the inner circle is the security/comfort zone to which individuals must be able to retreat from time to time. The partners are each in the other's security zone, and in this context should play their part accordingly. It will not help the relationship if, in times of need, the security zone is made uncomfortable by the introduction of additional problems. These will have to be tackled at some time but they should not be allowed to dominate this central space.

The majority of homicide is committed by family or "friends" of the victim. This is because their interaction is close to their egocentres. Any offence, hurt or injury is, therefore, committed from very close range, where the outer rings are not able to protect the individual and from where there is little room for further retreat. The egocentre is exposed and vulnerable.

7. Handling Interruptions (Reducing stress)
We have seen that emotions restrict our vision, and focus our attention on the subject of the emotion. Any interruption, to thinking activity which requires concentration, is likely to produce an emotional reaction. It is an interference which the egocentre will naturally wish to repel. Whether or not the interruption is dealt with objectively, the emotion will have narrowed the thinking perspective, and, temporarily at least, reduced its effective capacity. If you become aware of this, it is often better not to return immediately to the original subject, but rather switch to a less mentally demanding matter, allowing time for the emotional impact to subside.

CONCLUSION
We have seen in these last four chapters the reasons why people may think differently. If you listen to any debate or exchange of opinion, you will be able to identify the differences as being based on one of these:-

a)   Knowledge and experience;
b)   Status, position and allegiance;
c)   Substance;
d)   Emotion.

Understanding the cause of any difference is the first stage towards resolving it, or maybe avoiding it, and so this information should assist your dealings with other people.

Beware, however, of another aspect of emotion which needs to be mentioned. In general, people do not like to be proved wrong, particularly if the apparent error diminishes their egocentre. This will be seen as an attack which has to be repelled for the survival of the egocentre, and in these circumstances, any settlement of the difference will be very difficult. Two lessons may be drawn from this:-

1. In normal circumstances, do not try to press your opinion to a point which denies the other person space to manoeuvre.

2. Do not, yourself, feel threatened by the loss of an argument. Nobody can know everything. Look at the good points. You will have gained a new understanding which you may be able to use beneficially, *and* you will have earned a reputation of being open minded.

Above all, remember these words of Rudyard Kipling:

"If you keep your head when all about you
Are losing theirs and blaming it on you;
If you can trust yourself when all men doubt you,
But make allowance for their doubting too . . .
Yours is the Earth and everything that's in it,
And – which is more – you'll be a Man, my son!"

23
NOW LET ME THINK

There was once a vicar who used to travel around his parish on a bicycle, until one day it went missing. Despite extensive enquiries he could not trace it. He reported the loss to his bishop who suggested that his next sermon should be based on the Ten Commandments. "Place special emphasis on THOU SHALT NOT STEAL", said the bishop, "And this should prick the thief's conscience".

The following week the bishop was delighted to see the vicar riding his bicycle again.

"What did I tell you", he said.

"You were not quite right", said the vicar. "You see, I got to 'Thou shalt not commit adultery' and suddenly remembered where I had left it".

A fictitious story maybe, but the fact is that often our brains contain information which cannot be retrieved to order. It is locked away in memory.

Why is this?

It is because, generally, we are not programmed to recall information unless it is of vital importance to us. Our brains contain so much information that the majority of it has to be suppressed to leave room for current thinking. Imagine trying to think effectively if every piece of information in your head forced itself to your attention at the same time. It would be impossible. The purpose of memory is, therefore, to store for future use, information not required immediately. The problem is being able to retrieve it when it becomes necessary.

MEMORY STRENGTHS

An examination of the way our memories work, will help us to identify, and then improve, the areas in which we are normally most successful. These may be categorised as follows:-

1) Re-wind/Fast forward

In order for us to know who we are, and what we are, it is vital that we have some knowledge of what has gone before, and what we are planning to do next. At any moment, therefore, we have a re-wind facility which can tell us what we were doing ten minutes ago, two hours ago, two days ago, and even longer. This information is updated continually and, in order not to overload the system, earlier information is allowed to fade, the rate of decay differing according to its importance. Generally, the more trivial the information, the more quickly it will fade.

Fast forward allows us to plan for the future. We cannot always control it, and need to be flexible, but we all carry an expectation of what is to happen next. Whether it is finishing a spoken sentence, completing a journey, or planning some future event, our minds need to project forward to sustain continued activity. Without this, life would be like driving a car with rear-view vision only.

2) Repetition

If any of our thinking activities involve repetition, then as I explained earlier, our brains economise on effort by re-using information gained previously. The more frequent the repetition, the more deeply ingrained the information, the more readily available will be the re-call.

3) Welfare

The purpose of our brain is to aid survival and development, and so it is vital that any information relating to these matters is made available immediately it is required. Any matters of life and death, or those involving pain or pleasure, are, therefore, likely to surface quickly from memory.

4) Abnormalities

As we have seen in the development of the thinking structure, our brains organise information in an ordered fashion, so that patterns can be formed, and predictions made about unknown matters. New information has to be slotted into the structure, but occasionally, it is so out of line with established patterns, that a major review of the structure becomes necessary. Events of this nature are likely to be memorable.

5) *Associations*

Stored information is usually required from memory in blocks or chains, and not just as a single bit. Indeed, on its own, single bit information may well be useless. For example, think of the word "Table". Table what? Table tennis? Card table? League table? Table salt? Multiplication table? A collection of information is needed before it begins to have useful meaning.

The brain is very good at delivering this associated information. All it needs is a cue, or keyword, and it will offer a range of information which can be focused upon and selected consciously. It is as if the brain says, "When that information was used previously, you needed this as well". This is obviously a very complex exercise, and although it works very effectively, it cannot always produce every required piece of information to order. Hence the vicar's problem at the beginning of this chapter.

To examine the principle of *Associations* more closely, let us look at it in terms of the thinking structure described throughout this book.

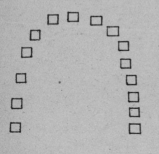

In this diagram the structure has been produced to deal with a specific, single subject. The blocks represent the relevant facts and experiences. When the subject is changed, a different set of blocks will be used to form a different structure.

For a moment, let us assume that the brain is not thinking about anything in particular, and has not therefore, produced a structure. The blocks of information may now be imagined as lying around in random order as illustrated in this diagram:-

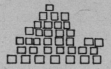

As soon as the brain focuses on a particular subject, the blocks form themselves into a pattern in a way which may be likened to iron filings responding to the influence of a magnet. In simple terms the pattern will look something like this

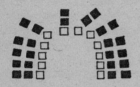

diagram. The white blocks represent the stored information which is relevant to the focal subject. The black blocks represent the other stored information.

The pattern into which these blocks form, places any information which is associated with the main subject in a cross-referenced line up.

For example, let us consider again the subject of CATS which I used for an exercise in chapter two. The structure would look something like this:-

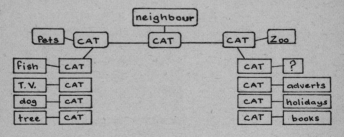

When you did this thinking exercise earlier, you uncovered numerous associations with cats, such as those shown in this diagram. These associations may be used in reverse. I have, for example, placed a question mark in one of the blocks in the previous diagram. If you now assume that the subject for this block is BIRDS, it may open up for you a further experience of cats which you did not previously consider. It can be seen from this that the use of association is a very important aid to memory.

Staying with the subject of cats, it will be impossible for you to extract from your mind *every* single piece of relevant information. For one reason, you will not have programmed yourself to produce the information; for another, the subject is too vast, and thirdly, it is unlikely that you would ever want to remember everything you know about cats. You will be able to recall the most important, central features, without difficulty, but will be less successful at the vague edges. Furthermore, as you do not know how much information on the subject you have stored away in your brain, you will not know how successful you have been in retrieving it. You may find it easier to answer specific questions about cats, because the questions themselves will focus your attention and limit the area of search for an answer.

PLANNING FOR IMPROVEMENT

As we have seen, the more important the information, the more likely it is to be remembered. There is a limit, however, to what may be regarded as important, and clearly it is not possible to remember everything which passes through the brain. Indeed, there is no point. The late Jacob Bronowski, the brilliant scientist, writer and broadcaster, once claimed that he never attempted to remember any information which he could conveniently write down. The same applies to information contained in textbooks or computer data files. It is often sufficient to know of its existence and whereabouts, and how it can be accessed.

For information which *does* need to be committed to memory, successful retrieval depends on the way in which the information is stored originally. This is why old people with fading memories have a better recollection of the distant past, than of more recent events. The earlier information was stored more effectively.

The time to plan for improved memory is, therefore, at the input stage. This may be at the point of initial learning, or at a later stage when information is recalled for revision. There are several methods of storing information for easy retrieval, and I will now deal with some of these. They make use of the memory strengths mentioned earlier.

1. MEMORY TECHNIQUES

Remember, if re-wind information is not required, it will fade. The brain, therefore, has to decide which information to retain, and this will normally be limited to that which directly affects welfare, involves abnormalities, or is likely to be needed again. It recognises the latter by repetition and this can, therefore, be used as a memory technique:-

a) Repetition

The learning stage is repeated over and over again until the information is firmly imprinted on the mind. This method, when used consciously, is generally used for relatively small amounts of important information such as multiplication tables and the alphabet. The information is stored at a primary level and can usually be retrieved instantly. Unfortunately however, because of the time and effort required at the input stage, there is a limit to the amount of information which can be stored in this manner. Nevertheless, the method is very useful, both in its own right, and as a basis for more complex mental activity.

b) Review

In the case of more extensive material, it may not be practical to repeat the entire learning process. Nevertheless, some form of review will be beneficial. This will be most effective immediately following the initial learning experience while the new information is still contained in backwind memory. A review at this stage will suggest to the brain that the information is likely to be needed again and is, therefore, worthy of retention. This will extend the life of the information within the re-wind, and a further review a short time later should convince the brain that the information is important enough for storage in long term memory. The first review tells the brain that the information is likely to be needed again, and the second review proves the point.

2) KEYWORDS AND ASSOCIATIONS

The use of association is a very powerful aid to memory. We

have seen, for example, how associations with *cats* expanded our recall of this subject. Keywords carry additional information with them, and, when produced as summarised headings, can be used to help memorise extensive subjects. The technique is, first to summarise the information, and then summarise that summary until you are left with the keywords. The keywords themselves can be committed to memory using the repetition method, or each one can be associated with the next in chain fashion.

3) STEPS AND PATTERNS

Retrieval from memory will be helped if the information to be absorbed has a logical progression or pattern. For example, traditional poetry, with a regular metre and rhyme, is much easier to remember than an equivalent passage of prose. Advantage may be taken of this by making a pattern or poem out of the information to be stored. This is, of course, an important method in teaching young children. You probably know the number of days in each month from the rhyme – "Thirty days hath September, April, June, and November, etc . . ."

In these cases, the brain does not produce the required information instantly, even though it is stored at a primary level. The pattern has to be followed through in stages, each stage providing the cue for the next, until the required piece of information is obtained.

Visual patterns also come into this category. In these cases it may not be necesary to search through the stored information in linear fashion. Instead, it may be possible to focus immediately on the part of the pattern which holds the required information. For example, think about your knowledge of your local neighbourhood. It would be difficult to recall *everything* you know about the area, and yet you could select *any* two locations and, from your memory, give accurate instructions for travel from one to the other. This principle may be used to commit other patterns of information to memory.

For example, suppose the subject is car mechanics. Each part of the subject is stored in a memory box, and the collection of boxes is formed into a pattern which may be likened to a family tree, as illustrated, or may be shaped like a plan or map:-

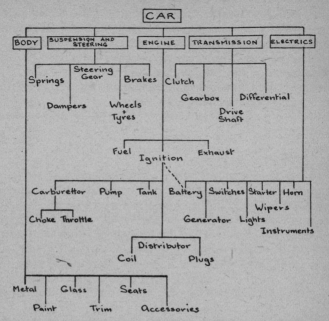

The advantages of this are firstly, that you can see the context of each part in relation to the whole, which increases understanding and therefore, memory. Secondly, you will have a finite view of the subject, and will more easily be aware of any ommisions. Thirdly, you will be able to focus on specific parts of the subject, in a similar way to that described in connection with your knowledge of your local neighbourhood.

Clearly, it will not always be possible to start with an overall view. The learning exercise may begin with the parts, and build up to the whole. In these cases, the overall view will have to be taken by looking back over the subject during, or on conclusion of, the exercise.

4) MNEMONICS

This is a method of remembering a word or sentence, (at primary level), the initial letters of which assist the memory of the required information, (at secondary level). For example:-

a)   Richard Of York Gave Battle In Vain = Red, Orange,

Yellow, Blue, Green, Indigo, Violet.
Used to recall the sequence of the rainbow colours.

b) Some Men Have Even Jumped Over = Superior, Michigan, Huron, Erie, Niagara Falls, Ontario.
Used to remember the order of Great Lakes of America and the position of Niagara Falls, which have to be jumped.

There are many other mnemonics in common use and no doubt you have your own favourites. You can obviously make up your own as you think appropriate. You will, of course, have to make a conscious effort to remember the mnemonic and the translation, but it is easier to remember a sentence like "Richard of York", than it is to remember the precise sequence of the seven colours.

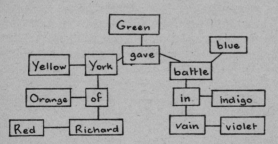

In diagrammatic terms, the structure for *rainbow* would look like this. The colours are produced from memory because of their association with the words in the key sentence. They would not otherwise be immediately available.

5) PICTURES AND WORDS
This method is similar to the previous one and is used for small pieces of information, word definitions or distinguishing features such as shown in these examples:-

a) StalacTites hang down as indicated by the letter T.

b) StationAry is stAnding :
StationEry = lEtters/Envelopes

   c)   MortgagOr = bOrrower : MortgagEE = lEnder.

   d)   When the moon is shaped like the letter D, it is
        Dawning : When it is shaped like a C, it is Closing.

You may make up your own examples but you must make a
positive effort to commit them to memory. Having stored them
in your memory in this way you will find that if, for example,
stalactite comes into your mind as a primary subject, the
secondary information will be triggered, and you will recall the
association with the letter T.

6) OTHER USES OF ASSOCIATION

a) Names

Association may be used to memorise the names of people.
Some visual or keyword link is made with the name which is
then committed to memory. This system can have its faults
however, and may lead to embarrassment. An example from an
old film, showed the star trying to remember a Mr. Crummock.
"Rhymes with stomach", he programmed himself, patting
himself in the appropriate place to reinforce the link. Later,
when he needed the recall, he patted himself once again and
said, "Goodbye, Mr. Kelly". Be careful!

b) Lists of Objects

More direct associations are preferable, and there is a system in
which an extensive list of required objects can be committed to
memory by forming a visual link with known keywords chosen
to rhyme with sequential numbers. The more outrageous the
visual association, the easier it is to remember because of the
principle of abnormalities mentioned earlier. Once programmed,
the objects may be recalled in sequence, triggered by the
keyword.

c) Memory Jogging

Because associated information is contained in boxes, it is often
possible to recall one of the bits by reference to any of the others
in the same box. For example, if ever you have misplaced
something, or forgotten where you last saw it, you may retrace

your steps, physically or mentally, to pick up some more easily remembered information which will then lead you to your target. Any one of the other pieces in the box can potentially open up the whole box. Remember the vicar's bicycle!

d)   Forward Planning
If ever you have to remember to do something in the future, you may write it down on a piece of paper, in a diary or personal organiser. The mental effort of writing will, in itself, improve the chances of future recall, but the aim is usually to rely on reference back to the written material as the memory jogger. This is not always possible, or practical. In these cases, the memory may be triggered by use of a programmed association.

For example, suppose you have to remember to call into the library on your way home. Think forward to what you will be doing at the moment you need to trigger your memory, and build into that image, an association with the library. An exaggeration will help as this will be seen as an abnormality, which is more easily recalled. Imagine, for example, a gigantic library book blocking your normal route at a critical point. When, at the future time, you arrive at this point, the associated information will be triggered and you will be presented with the image of the book.

CONCLUSION
And so back to the subject of this book, and the need to review. The intention has been to take you on a guided tour of your thinking process to help you identify any areas of weakness and seek opportunities for improvement. I hope you have been able to relate your own experiences to the examples I have used because this exercise is personal to you. It is your brain. The ideas, the memories, and the thinking processes are all yours. So think about it. You already have the necessary equipment. All you need is to put it to good effect.

Begin with a review. This is important because many of the subjects we have covered are inter-related and not easy to describe fully in linear form. A glance through the chapter headings will remind you of the various subjects that we have dealt with, and re-reading the Introduction should enable you to see the context of each part in relation to the whole.

Remember, it is for you to draw your own conclusions and make up your own mind, but above all else – use your brain.

APPENDIX I
ANSWERS TO PROBLEMS ON PAGES 52 & 53

1. The beggar is the woman's sister.
2. 7 Oranges.
3. Half way (after which he's coming out again!)
4. Survivors are not dead.
5. 31.
6. The North Pole.

APPENDIX II
FURTHER PUZZLES

1. For answer to castaway problem see page 156.

2. There are three books on a shelf, volumes 1, 2, & 3. Each book is 24mm thick, comprising 2cm thickness of pages, and 2mm for each cover. A bookworm eats its way from page 1 of volume 1, to the last page of volume 3. How far does it travel?

3. Two identical basins each contain identical volumes of sugar and salt respectively. A tablespoonful of sugar is taken from one basin, and mixed thoroughly with the salt in the other. An identical tablespoonful of the mixture is returned to the basin of sugar. Is there more sugar in the salt than there is salt in the sugar, or vice versa, or does each substance contain an identical volume of the other?

4. An LP record with a 12 inch diameter has a title label with a three inch diameter. Assuming the playing track starts at the outer circumference and continues to the centre label, and that there are ten grooves to the inch, how far does the needle travel during the playing of the record?

5. Two trains set out towards each other on the same stretch of track one hundred miles apart. One train travels at 25 MPH and the other at 50 MPH. At the instant both trains start, a bird flies from one train at 90 MPH down the track until it meets the other train. It then turns round immediately and flies back to meet the first train again. It continues to fly like a shuttle

between the two trains until they meet. Assuming no time is lost in making a turn, how far did the bird fly.

6.   In a far off country the coin of the realm is pure gold and weighs 100 grammes. The King has eight tax collectors who each collect different and unspecified amounts on behalf of their king. One of the collectors is a cheat. He files 10 grammes of gold off each of the coins he collects. This cannot be detected visually, but the king is aware that it is happening. One day, the king is visited by a foreign merchant, who offers him the use of his weighing machine. Unfortunately, the machine is the type which prints the weight on a ticket, and as the king has only one foreign coin with which to operate the machine, he is allowed only one weighing. How does he discover the identity of the cheat?

ANSWERS BELOW

APPENDIX III
ANSWERS TO PROBLEMS

1.   *Castaway:* The castaway goes to the southern half of the island and lights another fire to leeward. As the fire progresses, the castaway is able to follow, onto the area consumed by the second fire, which now forms a firebreak to protect him from the original fire.

2.   *Bookworm:* The answer is 28mm. Page 1 of volume 1 is to the right as you look at it on the shelf, and therefore immediately faces the cover which adjoins volume 2. Similarly, the last page of volume 3 is next to the cover which adjoins volume 2.

3.   *Basinful:* The basins each contain equal amounts of the foreign substance. Two explanations are:-

   a)   The final level in each basin is exactly the same as the start level. Therefore, whatever has been removed has been replaced by an exact volume of the foreign substance.

b) The second spoonful contained part sugar, part salt. If the sugar part of the second spoonful is deducted from the total amount of sugar contained in the first spoonful, the net amount of sugar taken to the salt will equal the amount of salt contained in the second spoonful.

4. *Needled:* The answer is four-and-a-half inches. As the record rotates, the needle moves from the outer edge to the centre label.

5. *Shuttlecock:* 120 miles. The trains are closing at a combined speed of 75 MPH. It will therefore take 1 hour 20 mins for them to meet, during which time the bird would have flown 120 miles.

6. *Goldfingers:* The king stands the collectors in a line and takes from each a number of coins which equal his number in the line, ie. 1 from 1, 2 from 2, etc. He then weighs all these coins and checks by how many multiples of ten the answer falls short of the expected total of 3600 grammes. The answer will tell him the position in the line of the cheat.

In the same series . . .

TEST YOUR OWN MENTAL HEALTH

This self-evaluation workbook and self-cure programme has already helped thousands to assess their state of mind, and take positive and practical steps towards a better life. It also provides useful information for those seeking to help others in trouble.

POSITIVE SELLING

Richard Moss takes a light-hearted, yet down-to-earth, look at the qualities you must have for successful selling. He shows how vital it is to listen, as well as to talk, and how to gain your customers' respect. The *essential* handbook for salespeople everywhere.

THE RIGHT WAY TO APPLY FOR A JOB

Arthur Wilcox gives away the secrets of successful job-hunting. He shows you how to reply to job advertisements and fill in application forms so that *you* are invited for interview.

All uniform with this book

ELLIOT RIGHT WAY BOOKS, KINGSWOOD, SURREY, U.K.

OUR PUBLISHING POLICY

HOW WE CHOOSE
Our policy is to consider every deserving manuscript and we can give special editorial help where an author is an authority on his subject but an inexperienced writer. We are rigorously selective in the choice of books we publish. We set the highest standards of editorial quality and accuracy. This means that a *Paperfront* is easy to understand and delightful to read. Where illustrations are necessary to convey points of detail, these are drawn up by a subject specialist artist from our panel.

HOW WE KEEP PRICES LOW
We aim for the big seller. This enables us to order enormous print runs and achieve the lowest price for you. Unfortunately, this means that you will not find in the *Paperfront* list any titles on obscure subjects of minority interest only. These could not be printed in large enough quantities to be sold for the low price at which we offer this series. We sell almost all our *Paperfronts* at the same unit price. This saves a lot of fiddling about in our clerical departments and helps us to give you world-beating value. Under this system, the longer titles are offered at a price which we believe to be unmatched by any publisher in the world.

OUR DISTRIBUTION SYSTEM
Because of the competitive price, and the rapid turnover, *Paperfronts* are possibly the most profitable line a bookseller can handle. They are stocked by the best bookshops all over the world. It may be that your bookseller has run out of stock of a particular title. If so, he can order more from us at any time—we have a fine reputation for "same day" despatch, and we supply any order, however small (even a single copy), to any bookseller who has an account with us. We prefer you to buy from your bookseller, as this reminds him of the strong underlying public demand for *Paperfronts*. Members of the public who live in remote places, or who are housebound, or whose local bookseller is unco-operative, can order direct from us by post.

FREE
If you would like an up-to-date list of all *Paperfront* titles currently available, send a stamped self-addressed envelope to
ELLIOT RIGHT WAY BOOKS, BRIGHTON RD.,
LOWER KINGSWOOD, SURREY, U.K.